Copyright for Schools:

A Practical Guide

THIRD EDITION

Carol Simpson

Linworth
PUBLISHING, INC.

Linworth Publishing, Inc.
Worthington, Ohio

Library of Congress Cataloging-in-Publication Data

Simpson, Carol Mann, 1949-
    Copyright for schools : a practical guide / Carol Simpson.— 3rd ed.
      p. cm.
    Includes bibliographical references and index.
    ISBN 1-58683-018-X (perfect bound)
     1. Fair use (Copyright)—United States—Popular works. 2. Copyright—United
States—Popular works. I. Title.

  KF3020.Z9 S57 2000
  346.7304'82—dc21

                                       00-048156

Published by Linworth Publishing, Inc.
480 East Wilson Bridge Road, Suite L
Worthington, Ohio 43085

Copyright 2001 by Linworth Publishing, Inc.

Series Information:
      From The Professional Growth Series

ISBN 1-58683-018-X

5 4 3 2

Table of Contents

Table of Contents *continued*

Table of Contents *continued*

Preface to the Third Edition

Copyright is no less an issue than it was when the first edition of this book was published in 1994. Teachers still receive little or no training in copyright compliance either in their university training or in their district staff development. Administrators may hear the word during school law classes, but the subject is not dealt with in depth. Librarians stand the best chance of learning the details of copyright during their library school training, but even their courses may gloss over important protections and permissions afforded schools and libraries.

All of these parties are generally astonished when a cease-and-desist letter (or a team of federal marshals) arrives on campus. The fact is that schools are being faced with copyright infringement actions at an unprecedented rate. Almost weekly, one hears of another school or library accused of copyright violation by a disgruntled employee, an irate student, a religious group attempting to strong-arm its political agenda, or a bounty hunter out for a sizable reward. Schools are highly visible targets because too often the personnel are unschooled and unaware of their obligations under copyright laws. Students often know more about the technological means to violate copyright than the adults know about the laws that are being violated. Schools are sitting ducks.

It's not that intentions aren't innocent, even noble. Schools seldom have the resources to purchase all the materials they would like to provide for their students. It's easy to rationalize a few copies here and there, a reward for hard work or perfect attendance, or just "borrowing" some images to make a Web page more appealing. After all, you aren't making any money on it, are you? Whom can it hurt? Who will know?

Copyright is as much an ethical as a legal issue. A teacher wouldn't think of walking through a lunch line full of students, taking a dessert, and leaving without paying for it. It would set a terrible example. It's dishonest. Yet the same teacher will display an attractive Web page for a class, then right-click on an especially attractive image and say, "We can just save this image to disk and use it whenever we like!" No notation that this is the work of someone else; no comment that one should ask permission before using another's work; no acknowledgement at all that a theft has just occurred.

Recent developments in copyright law such as the Sonny Bono Copyright Term Extension Act and the Digital Millennium Copyright Act have complicated the questions of what to do and how to do it. This edition of *Copyright for Schools* will address the aspects of the new laws that affect schools. In addition, I have included a feature that I call "Copyright Catechism." The dictionary defines the term "catechism" as learning through questions and answers. I've included representative questions about copyright that I have answered in my bimonthly "Copyright Question of the Month" columns (*Library Talk* and *The Book Report,* Linworth Publishing), and others that I am asked during presentations to educators and librarians. These aren't answers to specific, real-life quandaries and certainly don't substitute for competent legal advice, but they can guide you as you wrestle with your own copyright conundrums.

As I've stated in previous editions of this book, I am not an attorney, but I've been researching and writing about copyright laws and schools for 15 years. I became interested in the subject when I was presented with a video distribution system in the high school library where I worked. Knowing I was going to be "pushing the button" to send copyright-protected video throughout my building, I started researching my obligations under the law. I was astounded at the requirements that I had never learned but that put me and my faculty and administrators at risk. Fortunately, I had a supportive principal and an ethical faculty. All this isn't to say we were always "copyright clean," but we had a building expectation of compliance, we regularly trained our staff, and we monitored our materials and uses with an intent to comply with the various laws.

This monograph presents the safest position—that level of practice considered to be within legal limits by the most conservative application of the law. Certainly you might choose to stretch the recommendations and never be challenged. In some instances, the recommended practices might even be considered ultraconservative. The National Commission on New Technological Uses of Copyrighted Works (a.k.a. CONTU) Guidelines, for instance, if followed to the letter, might deny some user an arguably legitimate interlibrary loan. Some interpretations must necessarily be a judgment call, and they will be so noted.

Don't feel so frightened of copyright that you fail to employ every available opportunity to provide resources to your patrons. But the further afield you go from conservative interpretation, the stronger your rationale and your documentation should be. You will need both, if challenged. Don't confuse rationale with rationalization (in the Webster's New Collegiate Dictionary sense of "to attribute one's actions to rational and creditable motives, without adequate analysis of true motives"). Copyright violators frequently rationalize their acts. Such after-the-fact "explanations" will not stand up to legal scrutiny.

Above all, stand fast. The easiest road is not always the right and proper way. For many reasons, our government and the governments of dozens of countries around the world have protected authors and enabled educators to utilize intellectual property for research. The interests of one group influence and restrict the rights of the other. The balance is fragile. As educators and librarians, we want to provide whatever our patrons desire. As teachers and citizens, we have an obligation to model ethical and lawful behavior for our students. Make no excuses.

The information presented in this volume is not intended to substitute for qualified legal advice, but rather to help you determine if you need to consult an attorney for detailed guidance on a given situation. If you have any doubt that your activities are within the law, first read the law itself. It is available free of charge from the Copyright Office of the Library of Congress as Circular 99. The suggestions and guidelines in this book can help you decide if you are erring on the side of conservatism, or if you might be straying to the hazardous side of the street.

If in doubt, consult an attorney—preferably one who specializes in intellectual property (commonly listed as copyrights, trademarks, and patents, or some combination of those terms). Often specialists in educational law are unaware of the many layers of copyright protection. I know of several instances in which school district attorneys gave advice that was inaccurate, based on even the most liberal interpretation of copyright law. Many copyright attorneys will consult with you for an hour, providing authoritative legal advice, for about $200. When you're talking about professional integrity, $200 or $300 is a small sum to pay for a good night's sleep, and it can provide you with ammunition to take a firm stand against those who would have you play loose with the law.

All these rules and regulations may seem too complicated to be worth the trouble. After all, you haven't been caught so far, right? Cease-and-desist letters are on the rise, though, and reported cases of schools violating copyright—from computer software piracy (Los Angeles Unified School District) to photocopying workbooks (Beaumont, TX, Independent School District)—are only the beginning of the story.

Perhaps a parable will put the whole copyright problem into perspective.

Two second-graders are fighting over a ruler. One child is on each end of the ruler, pulling alternately.

"It's mine!" one yells, pulling the ruler.

"No, it's mine!" yells the other, pulling harder in the opposite direction.

The teacher steps in, claiming the disputed ruler. She determines to whom the ruler belongs, turns over the item, and sends him on his way. Taking the other child in tow, she scolds him sternly.

"You don't take what isn't yours without asking first!"

That's all copyright compliance is about: *You don't take what isn't yours without asking first.*

The ethics of theft are very clear. We don't take what isn't ours. Just as theft of another's property is against the law, theft of intellectual property is also illegal. Don't apologize. Copyright statutes are federal law. You need never apologize for obeying the law.

Carol Simpson

Acknowledgments

This book exists thanks to the persistence of Marlene Woo-Lun, and the dedicated, organized efforts of Linworth's stellar managing editor, Wendy Medvetz. A combination of a nagging mother and an award-winning cheerleader, she manages to make deadlines seem like celebratory events (especially when you meet them!). Special thanks go to Betty Morris, Maureen White, Kathy Patten, and Stephen Gillen, Esq., for their helpful comments in review of the text. My deepest thanks go to all the folks who have invited me to present copyright workshops to teachers, librarians, and administrators. These personal contacts have told me how many misconceptions, mistakes, and misapprehensions exist on the topic of copyright law. They also submitted many of the questions that you see in the catechism sections of the book. This book was written for them.

For my mother, Grace Pirrung

About the Author

Carol Simpson, Ed.D. is Assistant Professor in the School of Library and Information Sciences at the University of North Texas in Denton. A consultant for many school districts, she also is the editor of *The Book Report* and *Library Talk* magazines, publications of Linworth Publishing, Inc. She is the co-author of *Internet for Schools*, Third Edition (Linworth, 2000). She is a frequent speaker on copyright concerns and library technologies at conferences and workshops.

Chapter 1

What is Copyright?

As early as the beginning of the 18th century, publishers and authors in England had a legal right to control reproduction of their works. The United States based its original copyright law on the English version as well as providing protection through wording in the Constitution: " . . . [S]ecuring for limited times to authors . . . the exclusive right to their . . . writings . . ." (Article I, Section 8). George Washington signed the first U.S. copyright law, which has been rewritten several times over the ensuing years. The last major revision occurred in 1976, with minor modifications in the years since.

> *Q:* Do students own the copyrigtht on the works they create?
>
> *A:* Yes. Original student works are protected by copyright just as any other creative work. Because most public school students are minors, however, parents or legal guardians must grant permission in writing for schools to use student work in publications, exhibits, and other public venues.

U.S. copyright law (hereafter called "copyright law") covers all forms of expression as long as they are put down in some durable form—written on paper, recorded on tape, painted on canvas, or coded into a computer. The law uses the term "tangible medium of expression" to indicate what is called "fixation"– a requirement for copyright protection. In other words, an idea in your head is not protected by copyright, but if you write down that idea, or record it on tape, or otherwise put the idea into some permanently recorded format, your expression of the idea is now protected. The works may be prose, drama, dance, music, art, or sets of electronic instructions. The works don't even have to have a notice of copyright to be considered protected by the law. The old © symbol, so long required by older versions of the law, is no longer essential for copyright protection. In fact, one should assume that all works created on or after January 1, 1978, are protected by copyright unless shown otherwise. Each of us probably owns dozens of copyrights for letters, tests, papers, art, music, and other works we have created over the course of our careers. Kenneth

Crews related in an American Library Association online series on copyright: "If you can see it, read it, watch it, or hear it—with or without the use of a computer, projector, or other machine—the work is likely eligible for copyright protection."

If no notice of copyright is required for a work to be protected, why are notices included at all? Placing a notice on the work alerts potential users that the work is claimed as protected, and by whom. One would have a difficult time, indeed, claiming that she had no idea a work might be protected if there is a notice of copyright attached.

While most work created after 1978 is protected by copyright, an issue might arise about whose copyright it is. An interesting facet of copyright law known as "works made for hire" stipulates that works made within the scope of one's employment belong to the employer. There are many possible scenarios of this concept, so it isn't easy to define precisely. It would seem very clear that a newspaper journalist writing an article for the paper that employs him would not own the copyright in the article he writes. The newspaper employs that person to write articles, so the newspaper owns the copyright to the articles he writes within the scope of his employment. In a similar fashion, one could understand that a worksheet written by a fourth grade teacher for her science class would be prepared within the scope of her employment as a fourth grade teacher. In such an instance, the school would have a reasonable case asserting that the school owned the copyright in all the worksheets this teacher created for her classes. Should this teacher wish to compile all her worksheets into a book for sale, she would likely need clearance from the school for the use of the sheets.

The difficulty of obtaining that permission would vary with the school district and perhaps with the union contract under which the teacher works. A clause in teacher contracts regarding copyright ownership can forestall later disagreements. On the other hand, contract work may or may not be work-for-hire, depending on the contract wording. Specific types of work, such as parts of a collective work (e.g., book chapters), part of a film or other audiovisual work, a test, an instructional text, a translation, or a sound recording) can be considered works-for-hire but only if there is a written contract so stating. So a teacher who works over the summer under a supplemental, piecemeal contract to produce a curriculum guide might, in fact, own the copyright to the guide produced. The school would want to have a written agreement, signed by all parties, to assure that the copyright of the resulting product belongs, in fact, to the school. Some schools have encountered problems with this facet of copyright law when dealing with volunteers (adult or student) who work on school Web pages. Forewarned is forearmed.

What Is Not Protected by Copyright?

Understanding what is protected by copyright may be easier if one has a grasp of what is not protected. Circular 1, published by the U.S. Copyright Office, details the types of materials that cannot achieve copyright protection:

■ Works that have not been fixed in a tangible medium of expression, such as dance that has not been codified or recorded, or an improvisational speech that has not been transcribed or recorded. Opponents of university note-taking services such as Versity.com have emphasized that course lecture notes are protected by copyright because they are fixed, but the actual delivery of the lecture (unless the notes are read verbatim) is not protected. Professors who tape-record their lectures or who have them stenographically recorded may own the copyright on those lectures.

■ Titles, short phrases, names, common symbols, or designs (like a stop sign), slight variations on type styles, lettering, or coloring, or lists of ingredients.

■ Ideas, procedures, methods, discoveries, but descriptions or illustrations of these items may be protected by copyright.

■ Works containing only nonprotected material with no original authorship, such as plain calendars, lists of common facts, charts of measures.

> **Q:** We'd like to print and sell a recipe book for a fund-raiser. What copyright implications are there?
>
> **A:** Recipes consisting of lists of ingredients and simple assembly instructions may be freely reproduced as they are not protectable by copyright.

In addition to the materials listed above, works created by the federal government may not be protected by copyright. This prohibition involves works created by members of Congress or employees of federal agencies as part of their job responsibilities. Some federally funded projects written by nonfederal employees may have copyright protection, so it is always wise to investigate the copyright status of any work before making free use of it. The works of state and local government agencies may or may not be protected by copyright. Check thoroughly. Anything not protected by copyright, whether because it is ineligible for protection initially or because its period of protection has expired, is in the public domain (PD). Anyone may use material in the public domain in any way desired.

> **Q:** Why would I want to go to the trouble to register my creation?
>
> **A:** While registration is not required to achieve a copyright, it is needed before a suit is filed.

If he desires, the author of a copyright-eligible work can register the work in the Copyright Office of the Library of Congress <**lcWeb.loc.gov/copyright/reg.html**>. The set fee for registration of books and similar works is $30. (This fee is established by Congress and the Registrar of Copyrights, and is set through June 2002.) Registration is required prior to initiating any lawsuit to enforce one's copyright. Registration also confers some special benefits, such as being able to ask for statutory damages or attorney's fees in case of infringement. But whether registered or not, any work put down in tangible form after January 1, 1978, is protected. No notice is required on the items protected, nor is the copyright symbol (©) required, as had been the case before the most recent major copyright law overhaul.

These changes came about because the United States signed the Berne Convention, a worldwide treaty by which nations agreed to abide by each others' copyright laws. The Berne Convention simplified copyright enforcement because one now needs to know only the copyright laws of one's own country rather than those of hundreds of nations. For example, if you were to write a book and publish it in the United States, you would have to make appropriate registration only in this country. France, Germany, and Egypt (among many others) would protect your work as if it had been registered in all of those countries. This agreement also makes copyright compliance easier from a user's point of view in that we have to know the copyright laws of only one country–our own. Federal law protects the copyrights of all the Berne signatories. In most instances, we needn't learn the copyright rules of France, Germany, Egypt, or any of the other countries signing the treaty.

Rights of the Copyright Holder

From what is a work protected? Copyright law confers six rights on the creator of the copyrighted work:

- Reproduction (in copies or "phonorecords");

- Adaptation, or creation of derivative works;

- Distribution of copies or phonorecords (phonograph records) by sale, gift, rental, lease, or lending;

- Public performance of the work (for literary, musical, and dramatic works; pantomime and dance; and motion pictures and other audiovisual works);

- Public display (for literary, musical, dramatic, pantomime, and dance works; pictorial, graphic, and sculptural works; and individual images from motion pictures and other audiovisual material); and

- Digital audio transmission of sound recordings (such as music on Web pages and radio station simultaneous retransmission on the Internet.)

Some interesting interpretations have been made of these legal descriptions. A "phonorecord" is considered to be a copy. Such types of copies would exist if someone were to read a book onto tape. Copies don't have to be exact to be considered copies, so making a change in format such as recording a book or digitizing a photo could be considered to be making a copy or an adaptation or derivative work. Don't assume that the word "copy" means only photocopy. The law was written in this form long before photocopiers were in common use.

Derivative works are new works created from older, possibly protected works. When John Grisham writes a book, and someone turns that book into a screenplay, that person has created an adaptation or a derivative work. The same thing happens when a student modifies the work of an artist to create a new piece of art, or a teacher converts a cartoon into digital format for a PowerPoint™ presentation. All of these instances are derivative works.

A change of format is a key indicator of an adaptation problem. Other common derivatives are indexes, translations, concordances, abridgements, and recordings of musical works. Some derivative works, however, are entitled to copyright protection themselves (at least on their added-value portions and especially when the original work has fallen into the public domain), so one must not assume that all derivatives are under the control of the original copyright owner.

The right of distribution is limited by what is commonly called the "Right of First Sale." This corollary states that once the physical copy of a work has been sold, the right of distribution on that single copy no longer is held by the copyright owner. Without such termination of rights, a publisher could prevent a library from circulating books, a citizen or group from selling old paperbacks at a yard sale, or a person from giving a book to a friend as a gift. A group of recording artists challenged this right several years ago when they tried to boycott used CD stores. They claimed that the stores were making money on their previously sold works without paying royalties. The protest died, however, when it was pointed out that they had received their sales royalties the first time the CD was sold, and they no longer held any control over those copies.

A controversial and troubling case was decided in 1997. The decision held that a library could be found guilty of infringement if it allowed researchers to use materials only on the premises. The materials were later found to be illegal copies, and the library was held to be responsible for distribution even though the copies were never removed from the library. (Hotaling v. Church of Jesus Christ of Latter Day Saints, 118 F.3d 199 (4th Cir. 1997)) Such a ruling makes libraries, in particular, take care that the materials they hold are legitimate.

The restrictions on public performance and display apply to many more situations than you might imagine. Showing the page of a book in class is a public display, as is posting artwork on the class bulletin board or even in a museum. Section 109 (c) of the law allows legally acquired copies of artwork to be displayed where those works are located, so you can hang a poster you have purchased, or you can display the books that the library owns, but you can't scan those into a Web page and display them around the world.

The limited exception to public display does not carry over into public performances, however. Public performances include showing films or videos; playing musical or dramatic records, CDs, or tapes; showing a Web page or a computer program screen to a class. While doing these things for personal use, in a private place, is within the fair use of an item (see section on Fair Use for more details), displaying or performing them publicly is another issue entirely.

What Is "Public"?

The law is specific, yet vague, when defining what constitutes a public performance or display. At issue is what, exactly, is "public"? The law defines a public performance as: "[T]o perform or display it at a place open to the public or at any place where a substantial number of persons outside of a normal circle of a family and its social acquaintances is gathered; or to transmit or otherwise communicate a performance or display of the work to a place specified by [the previous] clause or to the public, by means of any device or process, whether the members of the public capable of receiving the performance or display receive it in the same place or in separate places and at the same time or at different times."

Schools, certainly, can meet the definition as described above. No matter that we may want our students to view the school as "home" and "family-like," that fact remains that the school is a public place. Gatherings such as Boy Scout or PTA meetings would be considered public.

Works must have at least some degree of creativity or originality to be considered eligible for copyright protection. In 1991, the Supreme Court held that a traditional alphabetical telephone directory did not contain enough original, nonfactual materials to be considered eligible for copyright protection (Feist Publications, Inc. v. Rural Telephone Service Co., Inc., 499 U.S. 340, 1991).

The creator of the work owns the previously listed (page 4) six rights subject to limitations called "fair use." These six rights are, in effect, property rights; hence, the term "intellectual property." The copyright owner may give, sell, or license any or all of these rights, either permanently or on any terms to which the owner and the requestor may agree. It is even possible (though unlikely) for six different groups or individuals to own different rights to the same work!

Should someone infringe, or violate, a copyright, a single infringement may violate all six rights at the same time, but copyright is violated if even one of the six exclusive rights is abridged.

> **Did You Know?**
> All transactions transferring copyrights must be done in writing. Verbal agreements and simple statements such as "I claim no copyright in this work" are not binding unless they are signed.

Moral Rights

In 1990 Congress granted a new group of rights called "moral rights" that apply to certain types of visual artwork (painting, sculpture) produced in limited quantities (fewer than 200). In such cases, the author can require that his name remain with the object. In addition, the artist has some power to prevent his artworks from being defaced or destroyed. In one case a sculptor successfully sued a municipality when a large sculpture, installed on city property, was destroyed without his permission.

Duration and Conditions of Copyright

How long is a work protected? It depends on when it was created. The time of creation (or registration) determines if, and how long, a work is protected. Works created on or after January 1, 1978, are protected for the life of the author plus 70 years. If there are two or more authors, the work is protected for the life of the longest-lived author, plus 70 years. For works of corporate authorship, works for hire, and pseudonymous works, copyright protection extends for 95 years from the date the work is published or 120 years from the date it was created, whichever is shorter. Works published before 1923 are currently in the public domain. Those created prior to 1923 but never published may still be protected. Those created between 1923 and 1978 have varying periods of copyright protection. Laura Gasaway, librarian and law professor, has a Web page that explains when works pass out of the protection of copyright: **<www.unc.edu/~unclng/public-d.htm>**

Q: *Is the Bible considered public domain? If it is copyright-protected, who would own the copyright?*

A: The answer depends on the version. The King James version is in the public-domain– at least in the original translation. New translations may still be protected. Check the copyright date of the version you are using. Anything before 1923 is public domain. (Watch out for "enhanced" versions, though. The Bible text itself may be public domain, but the notes are copyright protected.)

How do you know if a work is protected? If a work was created in the United States after January 1, 1978, you know that the work was automatically protected by copyright at the moment it was "fixed" or written down, saved to disk, painted on canvas, or otherwise given durable form. There need be no "C-in-a-circle" mark or other notification of copyright, and the author need not have registered his work with the copyright office in order to own a life-plus-70 years copyright on the work.

For works created prior to January 1, 1978, a notice of copyright and registration with the copyright office were required to obtain valid copyright protection. Those works published without such notice were considered to be in the public domain–without formal copyright protection. For various other periods of time back to 1923, different rules and durations of copyright protection were in effect. See Laura Gasaway's chart at the Web site above for more detailed information. For unpublished works (private letters and diaries, manuscripts, family photos), however, notice and registration are not required, and the works retain their copyright protection for many years.

Since notice of copyright can be an important factor in determining responsibility for willful infringement, the Digital Millennium Copyright Act (DMCA) included strict new regulations regarding removal of what the act calls "copyright management information." Such information can include the actual copyright notice affixed, but also might include the names of the author and copyright holder, performers, writers, title, or other information.

Removal of copyright information will be especially important in cases of library photocopying. Under previous iterations of the law, a simple notice of possible copyright was sufficient to protect a library from complicity in copy infringements. Most libraries used a basic ALA-approved stamp: *Notice: This material may be protected by Copyright Law (Title 17 U.S. Code)*. Under DMCA, this warning would no longer be sufficient. If a work's copyright notice can be found, the entire notice must be included (either photocopied or hand written) with the copies. If no copyright notice can be found on the work, the former stamp is sufficient.

The process for registering a copyright is set out by type of material. All require a $30 registration fee, plus some copy of the material being registered. The requirements for the various types of copyright-eligible materials can be found online at **<www.loc.gov/copyright/circs/>**.

Public Domain

Since the creator owns the copyright, some or all of these rights may be sold, rented or leased, given or abandoned, just as one may do with physical property. Most book and article authors sign the copyright of their works over to the publisher of the work in exchange for fees or royalties. Before the signing of the Berne Convention, authors who did not wish to claim their right of copyright could donate their work to what is called the "public domain." Works in the public domain have no copyright restrictions at all.

Once an item is identified as in the public domain, one may make any use of it one desires. It may be copied, scanned, adapted, distributed, displayed, or performed as one wishes. Items may be marked as in the public domain (most commonly computer software and graphics) or may fall into public domain when the copyright expires.

Since the Berne Convention, works are automatically protected by copyright from the moment they are created, causing problems for those who do not wish to claim copyright on their creations. Disposal of one's rights under copyright can be accomplished only with a signed instrument, but to whom would one convey such notice? Transfer of copyright is a standard contractual transaction, but abandonment is another matter entirely. For those who do not wish to profit from their works, a viable option is to mark the material as royalty-free; however, such notice still does not convey loss of rights to the product.

> *Q:* I want to use a book but it is out of print and the publisher is out of business. Is the book now free to reproduce?
>
> *A:* Out of print is not the same as out of copyright (or public domain). If the work is (or might be) still protected by copyright based on its original date of publication (after 1923), *someone* may own the copyright. Use the copyright office files to locate the current owner for permission.

How does one find out if a work is in the public domain? Good research is the only way if the work isn't marked as public domain. Of course, works published before 1923 would have no protection under copyright (unless a new edition has been released). Shakespeare's plays, for example, aren't protected by copyright in their original form as they were published before 1923. If notes, commentary, or background information have been added to the play, however, those portions of the works may be covered by copyright (provided they were written after 1923), as would be contemporary illustrations. Some unpublished works—previously protected under common law copyright but now released under new legislation—will start entering the public domain in 2003 if their 70 years-after-death period has lapsed. Watch for diaries, photographs, and manuscripts to appear starting in that year.

A journal is available to help you track down items falling into the public domain. Public Domain Report (also available online at <pubdomain.com>) identifies music, literature, plays, films, art, and children's literature that have entered the public domain. The publisher will also do custom research for a small fee, and can provide public domain sheet music, as well.

The U.S. Copyright Office **<lcweb.loc.gov/copyright/>** registration records are public. They may be searched online, or one can pay the researchers at the office to conduct research for an hourly fee.

Caveat: Just because a work has no notice of copyright does not mean that the work is in the public domain. In fact, because the World Wide Web was created after 1978, many things you see on the WWW are protected by copyright unless they are created by some entity forbidden to hold copyrights (such as government agencies) or are a reprint of some public domain work such as old (pre-1923) literature.

Law vs. Guidelines

The copyright law, Title 17, United States Code, Public Law 94-553, 90 Stat. 2541, as amended, gives schools and a limited number of other users special exceptions to the strict legal copyright requirements. The purpose of these limited exceptions to the exclusive rights of copyright holders is to advance knowledge and scholarship. These special exceptions are called "fair use." Since the text of the law was too vague to be of much help in deciding if a particular use was permissible, the House of Representatives and the Senate held hearings to determine an equitable balance between the rights of copyright owners (who may or may not be the actual creators of the copyrighted works) and those of the general public.

The hearings resulted in a set of guidelines (often referred to as the "Congressional Guidelines" or "fair use guidelines" (**<www.musiclibraryassoc.org/ Copyright/guidebks.htm>**) that, while they are not law, are interpreted to be the Congress' intent in enacting the law. The courts have taken this statement of intent into account when deciding cases of copyright infringement. The House report on congressional intent was quite explicit on the amount and types of copying that could be considered fair use. These specific limits are discussed in the section on fair use.

Penalties and Liability

Should a person choose to ignore the law, the penalty for copyright infringement is not a minor inconvenience. Damages can be actual or statutory, depending on how the suit is filed and whether the copyright to the infringed work was registered before the infringement commenced. Statutory fines range from $750 to $30,000 per infringement, with each individual work constituting a separate act of infringement. A limited exception permits truly unwary offenders (also called "innocent infringers") to have their fines reduced to as little as $200 per work infringed, but such reduction in penalty is at the discretion of the court.

To qualify for such an exception, the defendant would have to present a strong case that he truly believed, with reasonable justification, that his use of the work was within fair use. If the court decides the infringement was knowledgeable and intentional, statutory damages can run as high as $150,000 per instance. Legal fees and court costs can escalate the true cost of losing a copyright infringement case, since a defendant judged guilty may be required to pay the copyright holder's attorney fees and court costs as well as the statutory penalties. Of course, there is no cost that can be put on lost sleep and worry.

Most copyright suits are civil matters, but in 1992 the penalty for criminal infringement of computer software copyright (commonly called "piracy") was raised to felony status, with fines up to $250,000! Making as few as 10 illegal copies with a total value of $2,500 or more worth of software is a criminal offense. For complete information about potential penalties and liabilities, see Chapter 5 of U.S. copyright law at **<www.loc.gov/copyright/title17/chapter05.pdf>**. For more surprising information about copyright, See Brad Templeton's "Ten Big Myths About Copyright" **<www.templetons.com/brad/copymyths.html>**.

Here are examples of three types of infringement:

- Innocent infringement. A teacher reads in a journal that an item has fallen into public domain and makes copies. In truth, the journal confused two items of similar title.

- Standard infringement. A librarian makes copies of an article for a class many months in advance without making any attempt to contact the copyright holder and obtain permission.

- Willful infringement. A principal asks permission to reproduce copies of a journal article for the faculty and is denied. He makes the copies anyway without a reasonable basis to believe he didn't need permission.

When a court finds that a copyright has been infringed, it may take one of several courses of action. An injunction prohibits the supposed copier from making further use or copies of the purloined work. This penalty is used primarily in cases of large-scale use or copying for profit. The court might also impound or destroy illegal copies. Of course, monetary damages are generally sought, and those damages may be actual (true monetary losses) or statutory (defined by law). Actual damages are usually requested only in large-scale piracy cases, since the copyright holder must prove lost profits. Statutory damages are the type most often requested in suits against schools and school personnel. Court costs may be assessed to the loser of a copyright action. Attorneys' fees of the prevailing party may also be charged to the loser of an infringement suit, but a prevailing plaintiff will get them only if the copyrighted work in dispute has been registered with the copyright office within the time frame prescribed by law. A prevailing defendant will get fees and costs whether or not the copyright was filed in a timely manner.

If someone in the district or building violates copyright, that person pays the fine, right? Well, not exactly. Copyright watchdog groups report the results of infringement actions, both as spoils of victory and warnings to those tempted to skirt the law. Most of the reported cases indicate that the classroom teacher or librarian is only the beginning in naming liable parties. Many suits go right up the chain of command, from librarian, to principal, to curriculum director, to superintendent, to the board of education under the assumption that these parties are aware of and responsible for the actions of their employees.

Two supplemental forms of liability enter the picture at this point. School employees can be considered contributory infringers if they helped the copier do the illegal act or if they were in a position to control the use of the copyrighted work. An example of such a situation would be a librarian who loaned two videocassette recorders and a set of patch cords, knowing they would be used to duplicate a copyrighted video. The librarian helped the copyright violator break the law by providing equipment he needed to do so. Why would someone want two VCRs and patch cords except to copy a video? In addition, the librarian may have provided the tape that was to become the illegal copy. If the librarian is in a position to refuse the loan, but makes the loan anyway, knowing its purpose, she may be considered to be a contributory copyright violator.

Employers would be vicarious lawbreakers if they had reason to know an employee was violating copyright but took no action. An example of vicarious infringement would be a principal who had been notified that a copyright violation was taking place but who took no action to stop the theft. Both vicarious and contributory copyright violators are just as liable as the person who actually made the copies or used the material.

The Librarian's Liability

We've all heard of "chain of command." Liability works in much the same way. If illicit copies are made on library-owned equipment, it's a good bet that the librarian who lent the equipment could be involved in the infringement action. A case could be made that the librarian knew (or should have known) that the event would be illegal. Only with the support of a strong copyright policy, good record-keeping, and thorough staff training would the librarian (and administrators) be able to prove that the copyright violator was acting as an individual.

The Principal's Liability

The principal, as the instructional and administrative leader in the school, must be aware of curriculum, student issues, staffing and personnel responsibilities, extracurricular activities, equipment and resources, and dozens of other issues affecting the building. Since he has such all-encompassing responsibility, it's understandable that when someone in the school breaks copyright law, the copyright owner will assume that the principal had at least passing knowledge of the event or control over those persons breaking the law. In either case, the principal could be at minimum a vicarious or contributory party to the offense. Such a possibility raises the likelihood that the principal will be named in any potential legal action against the school.

As you can see, the librarian and administrator are at some risk from the illegal activities of others. To that end, it is worthwhile to establish and maintain clear and thorough copyright records, and to inform school personnel and patrons of their obligations under the copyright law.

Administrators, once schooled on copyright, would probably appreciate notification when violations are observed. This isn't to say that the librarian or computer technician becomes the "copyright police." On the contrary, these staff members aren't charged with enforcing the copyright law. That falls to the FBI and the Justice Department. But the librarian and the technician are doing the students and staff of the school and the district a disservice to ignore a potentially damaging and embarrassing legal situation. Apprising a principal of a legal violation is akin to notifying her of a fire code violation so it may be corrected before the fire inspector arrives for inspection. Forewarned is forearmed.

How Is a School Prosecuted?

The first inkling a school might have of a copyright infringement might arrive in the mail. Many copyright owners choose to notify accused schools by sending a "cease-and-desist" letter. In instances where the copyright owner has good reason to believe that the accused might try to obliterate the evidence (such as removing contraband copies of computer software), federal marshals may arrive, unannounced, to seize evidence. Because most cases of copyright infringement are settled out of court rather than tried, there are few legal cases to draw upon. Making an inquiry on an educational listserv or at an educational conference will likely produce several educators whose districts have received cease-and-desist letters or have been investigated. Their experiences can guide you, though sometimes their stories are not positive ones.

In cases where the school is considered to be consistently violating copyright or where offenses are so numerous that the copyright owner wishes to make an example of the school or district, he will not be amenable to an out-of-court settlement. These "worst case" situations are not common. Being honest and open in an investigation can help you avoid the worst consequences.

Why Bother?

What is the point in keeping up with copyright? If a school can get away with violating the law, why not continue? The fact is that authors, producers, and publishers are increasingly aggressive about copyright enforcement. In fact, some producers require sales representatives or employees of subsidiaries to report observed copyright infringements as part of their jobs. Some of these companies even offer rewards for reporting violations and threaten termination if an employee observes a violation and fails to report it. Others, sometimes called "bounty hunters," make a living reporting violators and collecting rewards. One never knows if a parent visiting school for a conference or a doting aunt attending open house will find some violation of her employer's copyrights.

Groups with political agendas also pose a threat. A group seeking to block or remove a certain type of material from the school can simply observe violations of the company's copyrights, report them, and be sure the abused company will remove the material. They may even be rewarded by the company whose work they seek to censor. Cases have also been reported of students and disgruntled employees reporting schools for real or imagined copyright violations. Whether real or not, a copyright case causes untold grief and recrimination.

With armies of potential detectives in the field, sooner or later many illicit copiers will be caught. By the nature of their job responsibilities, school personnel might be considered active or passive participants in the violation, if proven.

The law provides a free ride for certain (not all) educational uses of copyrighted materials. Others must be paid for. If producers and authors can't expect to profit from their products because of illegal copies or uses, they will not be able to afford to make new materials. As educators, we have a vested interest both in modeling correct behavior and in obtaining new, high-quality educational materials. By abiding by fair use educational or library exemptions and encouraging our colleagues to do the same, we can help ensure a free flow of information into the hands of our patrons, assure a fair return to authors and educational publishers and producers, and set an example of responsible citizenship.

Chapter *2*

Fair Use

What Is "Fair Use"?

Fair use provisions of the copyright law grant particular types of users conditional rights to use or reproduce certain copyrighted materials as long as the reproduction or use of those materials meets defined guidelines. Fair use goes hand in glove with the intent of copyright "to promote the progress of Science and Useful Arts." As defined in the law, fair use balances the First Amendment free speech right with the rights of the author to control the use of his copyrighted work. When a court considers a claim of fair use, both the rights of the user and the rights of the author are considered. The burden of proving fair use falls to the educator using the material, so thorough knowledge of copyright law and associated guidelines is essential for librarians and educators using copyrighted works. As there is seldom a clear-cut fair use situation, it is incumbent upon the educator to know the conditions under which one may claim fair use.

The Educational Exemption

Section 106 of the copyright law codified in 17 U. S. Code defines six rights reserved exclusively for the copyright holder of a copyrighted work:

- Reproduction,
- Adaptation,
- Distribution,
- Performance,

- Display, and

- Digital audio transmission.

Copyright law, however, provides several instances in which reproduction of copyrighted items is permissible. These exceptions to Section 106 are considered the "fair use exemptions" and are found in Section 107 of the law. This section is brief enough to be reprinted here:

> Notwithstanding the provisions of sections 106 and 106A, the fair use of a copyrighted work, including such use by reproduction in copies or phonorecords or by any other means specified by that section, for purposes such as criticism, comment, news reporting, teaching (including multiple copies for classroom use), scholarship, or research, is not an infringement of copyright. In determining whether the use made of a work in any particular case is a fair use, the factors to be considered shall include:
>
> 1. The purpose and character of the use, including whether such use is of a commercial nature, or is for nonprofit educational purposes;
>
> 2. The nature of the copyrighted work;
>
> 3. The amount and substantiality of the portion used in relation to the copyrighted work as a whole; and
>
> 4. The effect of the use upon the potential market for or value of the copyrighted work.

These four factors are also known as the four tests of fair use. What the law is saying is that Congress intends to protect the rights of the author while still allowing legitimate educational and research uses of copyrighted materials. This is good news for schools and libraries. Beware, however, of the wording in factor 1: "Whether such use is of commercial nature or is for nonprofit educational purposes." This statement may seem like carte blanche for schools and libraries. In reality it is simply a statement that courts should take this factor into account in determining fair use in cases of possible infringement. Many school personnel will justify copying with the comment, "But it isn't like I'm going to make any money from the copies." In fact, making no financial gain from copies is not, in itself, a valid application of the fair use exemption.

The first test of fair use encourages educational use of materials, but it has been interpreted to favor "transformative" uses, such as putting a quotation in a term paper. A recent court case stated that making low-resolution thumbnail-sized copies of images available elsewhere on the Internet was a "transformative" use (Kelly v. Arriba Soft Corp., 77 F. Supp. 2d 1116 (C.D. Cal. 1999)). Even multiple copies of nontransformative uses can be acceptable in limited numbers. See the chapter on print materials for more details on multiple print copies. Keep in mind that, in the absence of specific guidelines, all four tests of fair use will be considered in determining an appropriate application of the fair use doctrine. Factor 1 is actually fairly insignificant when all four factors are applied to a given situation.

Factor 2 concerns the nature of the copy. What is being copied? Is it published or unpublished? (Note that out-of-print isn't the same as unpublished.) Is the work factual or creative? If you purchase a book of instructions or patterns, you would expect that fair use would allow you to follow the directions or pattern to create the item described. Factual materials get much more leeway in copying since simple facts cannot be copyrighted. "Simple facts" would include lists of names or telephone numbers, state capitals, street names, charts of distances or mathematics tables, simple outline diagrams, and similar compilations, unless unusually creative. A work of fiction, music, or art, however, would be less freely given to copying. Creative works are more highly protected. A court would consider exactly what is being copied when making a decision about fair use. Interpretation of this factor is generally straightforward.

Factor 3 delves into a gray area. How much of a work is "substantial" is a judgment call, and one that the court must make. Common sense would tell you that copying 10 pages from a picture book is a far more significant extract than 10 pages from a novel. The portion of a work that a court might declare to be "substantial" may be very small. In fact, in one landmark case, a 300-400 word excerpt of former President Ford's 454 page autobiography was held to contain the "essence" of the larger work, so copying that short excerpt was tantamount to copying the whole work. (Harper & Row Pub., Inc. v. Nation Enterprises, 471 U.S. 539, 105 S.Ct. 2218 (1985)). On the other hand, the Supreme Court held that the band 2 Live Crew could use a substantial part of the song "Pretty Woman," so how much is "too much" varies from case to case and court to court. Excessive copying can be determined only after taking into account the other three factors and the circumstances as a whole. Just remember that this is only one of four factors, so the use of a large portion of a work is not always a completely disqualifying point. In still another case, a teacher copied 11 pages of a 24-page handout from another teacher's copyrighted work on cake decorating. The courts held that the 11 pages were too much of the copied work to be classified as fair use, as well as the fact that the 11 pages comprised the most important sections of the work copied. The new work also competed directly with the original, since both were educational for a similar audience (Marcus v. Rowley, 695 F.2d 1171 (9th Cir. 1983)).

Congressional committees have worked to make specific recommendations about the number of words or pages that may be safely copied under the fair use exemption. The law tries to balance the needs of educators to access material with the needs of authors to sell their works. When in doubt, err on the conservative side. Use the minimum amount.

The last factor in the fair use section of the law concerns the financial impact on the copyright owner. The fair use analysis directs that the proposed copying or display should not adversely impact the market for or the value of the protected work. This factor alone is the most significant, and the previous three are derived in some degree from this concept. In simplest and most conservative terms, if copying would deprive an author of a sale, the copying is not within fair use exemptions. If there were any commercial intent, such as selling yearbooks or

Q: *I'd like to copy something from the Web to put on a local server. Since the Web author doesn't charge any money for the site, I'm not affecting the market for the work, right?*

A: Perhaps you are affecting the value of the work. If, for example, the author receives funding based on "hits" to the Web site, by copying the information and distributing it, you may impact the funding by drawing hits away.

band tapes or T-shirts, effect on a market is presumed (Crews, Message 23, Oct. 26, 1998).

A copyright attorney once described this concept with this question: What would happen if thousands of people copied this material in the same way? Courts actually consider potential damage, rather than actual damages, when weighing this factor. Making copies of an editorial cartoon from the newspaper would probably not deprive the publisher of a sale, since few people would purchase the paper just for the editorial cartoon. Copying workbook pages to avoid having to purchase 30 copies of the workbook obviously deprives the author or publisher of 30 sales. The fact that the teacher or school makes no financial gain on the transaction is secondary, as is the fact that one workbook page is a tiny fraction of the whole. The workbook is intended to be consumable; sales of multiple copies are supposed; hence, circumventing this expectation is not appropriate use. The potential financial impact of the copying, if many people were to make similar copies, will be the single most significant consideration in a determination of the fair use exemption.

Congressional Guidelines

Q: *As English coordinator, I would like to require all the high school English teachers to copy and distribute an editorial from the local newspaper to use as a standardized test-writing prompt. Since this is a small newspaper, would this be permissible?*

A: This small copying would be acceptable if the classroom teacher were making the copying decision, (see question 1). Because this copying is being directed by a higher authority, such copying is not permitted under the fair use guidelines.

Because the four factors cited in Section 107 left much to subjective interpretation, Congress produced much more specific explanations of the law. These Congressional Guidelines **<www.musiclibraryassoc.org/Copyright/guidebks.htm>**, as they are called, are not law, but were written to indicate legislative intent and are used as benchmarks against which copyright infringement is gauged. These guidelines were developed primarily for print materials. While Congress placed specific limits and restrictions based on the format of material, it also imposed some general tests for all educational uses of copyrighted works. These tests are more concrete and easier to apply to educational and library copying than are the fair use factors. The additional tests are those of brevity (defined by specific lengths and numbers of items), spontaneity (see following questions), and cumulative effect.

If you copy or display any part of a work under the fair use exemption, you should be able to answer yes to both of the following questions:

1. Copying (or display) is at the instance and inspiration of the individual teacher, and

2. The inspiration and decision to use the work and the moment of its use for maximum teaching effectiveness are so close in time that it would be unreasonable to expect a timely reply to a request for permission.

Essentially this restricts educators from having materials (or television programs) copied in anticipation of demand. All requests for duplication, whether photocopies or off-air taping, must come directly from the teacher involved. In other words, an administrator, department head, librarian, or other person in a position of authority may not direct teachers or librarians to copy materials under the fair use exemption.

Those same authorities may not forecast that teachers will request copies of a particular resource and cause that item to be copied so it will be available, on the chance that a teacher might ask for it. This type of situation frequently occurs when a principal or librarian sees that a scheduled television program would relate to some curriculum. The educator decides to copy the program in expectation that teachers will ask for the program after the fact. In order to comply with the fair use guidelines, the request for taping must come from the teacher who wishes to use the program. This is often described as a "bottom up" rule: The person at the point of use (the classroom) is the one who must request the copying.

The second test requires that all fair use duplication must happen so closely to the date of anticipated use that one could not reasonably expect a response to a request for permission. In other words, copying two months before the expected date of use would not qualify as fair use because the teacher could reasonably expect to have a response to a request for permission in that amount of time. Here are some typical examples:

Q: As librarian I like to have materials on hand. I know my teachers will want a tape of a particular TV program. May I tape the programs knowing they will ask for it?

A: Taping in anticipation of request is not permitted. You can, however, notify the teachers in advance and suggest they fill out a taping request so you can have the tape for them when they need it.

Q: As a principal, I want to have teachers read the latest professional materials. I propose having my faculty maintain a notebook of articles that I select, but they photocopy. Is this permitted since I will not be doing the copies?

A: Probably not. As the teachers' supervisor, you may suggest they read the articles, but the decision to copy the materials must be left up to the teachers themselves.

Permissible:	Not Permissible:
In a news magazine, a teacher reads an article that would fit in nicely with her new unit of study. She requests the teacher aide to copy the article for her to use in class within the next two weeks.	A curriculum coordinator directs all the English teachers to photocopy a newspaper editorial to use as an example of persuasive writing.
A teacher finds a Web site appropriate to the lesson she will teach this week, and she displays it for the class.	A technology director seeks out educational Web sites and copies their contents to a school's server for long-term future reference.
A teacher sees a chart in Ranger Rick that fits in with her current unit on dinosaurs. She makes a transparency of the chart to use with her class the next day.	A teacher sees a chart in Ranger Rick that will fit in nicely with her unit on dinosaurs next semester. She makes copies for the class and puts them in a file for future use.

Some additional very specific restrictions are imposed on audiovisual materials—television and video in particular. The specific regulations will be discussed in the sections on audiovisual works and off-air recording. In general, however, all use of radio, television, and video must be directly related to the teaching objective. Even programs that hold general educational or cultural value cannot be used without prior permission unless they relate to a specific teaching objective. Use of film, audio, video, or television for reinforcement, entertainment, or reward is prohibited unless public performance rights were purchased for the program.

Fair Use Recommendations

As you can see, many of the "don'ts" listed above are common practice in many libraries and schools. The fact that these practices are routine means they will be just that much more difficult to break.

Here are some suggestions for guidelines to assure fair use compliance in libraries, school buildings, and school districts:

Libraries:

Teach (preach?) copyright principles to library patrons. Speak of copyright obligations as you provide materials to patrons and as you teach use of various media. Even elementary students are not too young to understand the obligations of copyright.

Post copyright notices on copy machines, video recorders, tape recorders, computers, and any equipment capable of making copies of any sort. Put copyright warning stickers on commercial videotapes and circulating copies of computer software. Be prepared to explain the legalese.

Request permission. Have a form letter ready for permission requests, fill-in-the-blank, if possible.

Track copyrighted material that passes through the library. Television programs taped at home, rented videos, and the like should have signed agreements from faculty members stating that the materials comply with fair use. Document educational exemption with lesson plans that tie the material to the curriculum and the lesson at hand.

Keep records. All material (especially audiovisual) purchased for the building collection should be tracked for copyright and public performance clearance. Notations on the shelf list or computer record of each piece with clearance should suffice. MARC tag 540 is designated to hold copyright-specific information regarding individual items. See <lcWeb.loc.gov/marc/bibliographic/ ecbdnot2.html#mrcb540> for details. Retain a file of permissions and purchase orders documenting acquired rights.

School Buildings:

Encourage and model copyright law compliance.

Monitor use of copy machines. Wholesale copying is likely to violate copyright.

Promote original materials. Using opaque projectors to enlarge graphics, coloring books, greeting cards, illustrations, cartoons, and other copyrighted material is out of compliance unless you've gotten specific permission. An exception would be simple map outlines. If teachers model behavior that emphasizes duplicating the works of others, how can we expect students to utilize their higher order thinking skills to create innovative works?

Require that lesson plans document tie-ins for copyrighted print and audiovisual materials. Requiring administrative pre-approval for classroom video use can help reduce both copyright infringement and poor teaching.

Distribute written guidelines and expectations for faculty and any staff involved with duplication of print or audiovisual materials. Many staff members violate copyright out of ignorance, but lack of knowledge of the requirements of copyright is not an acceptable defense if one is accused.

Verbalize high expectations of the staff. Remind them that their actions are being watched by their severest critics—their students.

School Districts:

Write and adopt a comprehensive copyright policy.

Appoint a copyright officer for the district to advise staff on complex issues in concert with the district's legal counsel.

Maintain histories of public performance rights purchased.

Provide in-depth training to all school district employees who deal with copyrighted materials—teachers, administrators, and clerical staff.

Encourage district's legal counsel to consult on copyright concerns if he is trained in this area. Intellectual property is a legal specialty. If your district's attorney does not have training in or an interest in this aspect of the law, request consultation with a specialist.

Advertise and conduct software copyright audits to monitor compliance. Such audits will give district-level administrators an idea of the vulnerability of the building or district. Read more about audits in the chapter on computer software.

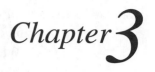

Print Materials

E ver since the first copyright statute was enacted, the primary focus of the law has been to protect the authors and publishers of books and other print media. Until the invention of the printing press, no one worried much about illegal copying or distribution that might injure a copyright holder. Copying was so tedious and labor-intensive there were few legal copies and fewer illegal ones. Cheap and easy mass printing made theft or misappropriation of an author's works much easier.

In today's world, modern technology has made reproduction and distribution of almost any work or image nearly instantaneous. Digital copies are virtually indistinguishable from the original. Nothing in print is safe from an intent copier. For that reason, legislators made the law quite restrictive, putting all copying and distribution of copyrighted works under the control of the copyright holders. Copyright holders may make all determinations about copies and uses of the materials they have created.

Libraries, though, have specific exemptions under the copyright law. If libraries didn't have a limited exemption to the distribution prohibitions, they couldn't lend books and other materials to patrons. There are other exceptions for libraries. For example, if a library owns a copy of a book, and a page is damaged beyond use, it is within the library uses granted under Section 108 of the copyright law to photocopy and tip in the missing page from another copy. In fact, it is within the rights granted libraries to copy an entire book when the original is lost, damaged, or deteriorated beyond use, if an unused replacement cannot be purchased at a reasonable price.

Libraries also have certain protections against being sued for copyright infringement when contraband copies are made on unsupervised copiers in the library. "Unsupervised" could be construed to mean those coin-operated copiers available for public use in the library. The library staff has no responsibility for the making of copies on these machines other than perhaps stocking the machine with paper and occasionally unjamming the works.

When the library staff becomes involved in actually making the copies, additional requirements arise. Since notice of copyright can be an important factor in determining responsibility for willful infringement, the Digital Millennium Copyright Act (DMCA) included strict new regulations regarding removal of what the act calls "copyright management information." Such information can include the actual copyright notice affixed, but also might include the names of the author and copyright holder, performers, writers, and title. Removal of copyright information will be especially important in cases of library photocopying. Under previous iterations of the law, a simple notice of possible copyright was sufficient to protect a library from complicity in copy infringements. Most libraries used a basic ALA-approved stamp stating *Notice: This material may be protected by Copyright Law (Title 17 U.S. Code)*. Under DMCA, this warning is no longer sufficient. If a work's copyright notice can be found, the entire notice must be included (either photocopied or handwritten) with the copies. If no copyright notice can be found on the work, the ALA stamp would be sufficient.

Schools have their own set of exceptions to copyright requirements, mostly granted under the "fair use" exemption. School libraries have the best of both worlds—the library *and* the educational exemptions. The fair use provision of the law allows limited copies to be made of print materials for several purposes, including teaching. However, not all copying for the purpose of teaching is considered fair use. Courts will consider four factors in determining fair use, considering each factor separately, but the cumulative effect of the four determines the outcome. The four factors are:

- The purpose and character of the use, including whether such use is of a commercial nature or is for nonprofit educational purposes;

- The nature of the copyrighted work;

- The amount and substantiality of the portion used in relation to the copyrighted work as a whole; and

- The effect of the use upon the potential market for or value of the copyrighted work. (17 U.S.C. 107).

If you intend to claim fair use, evaluate each of the four factors separately. Before you can make a solid case for fair use, you should be confident that at least three of the factors weigh in on the side of fair use.

As you can see, one could justify just about any type of school-based copying by citing one or more of these factors, and many educators try to do just that. However, the law mandates that *all four* factors be taken into account. Because this section of the law could be interpreted so broadly, Congress appointed a committee to establish guidelines on the reproduction of books and periodicals in order to clarify legislative intent of the various sections of the law. While the guidelines themselves are not law, Congress stipulated that individuals and courts should consider the guidelines when deciding the merits of copyright litigation. In that light, the congressional guidelines give a much better idea of the amount and types of copying permitted under fair use.

The guidelines state minimum standards of fair use; certain other types of copying may be permitted. Just exactly what those other types of copying are and how much is tolerated would depend on the judge and jury hearing the case. Yes, the final arbiter of what is permitted is a court of law. While you might be convinced that the pages you plan to copy fall under the fair use exemption, the copyright owner may have entirely different views. As stated in the introduction, the most conservative line is generally safe, whereas straying very far afield of these guidelines is an open invitation to litigation. One might make an analogy to driving. Going 31 miles per hour in a 30-mile-per-hour zone probably wouldn't merit a ticket, but going 50 miles per hour in the same zone would likely alert even the most laid-back patrolman. In a school situation, sometimes one is more comfortable giving teachers and students clear directions and numbers on which to judge appropriate behavior. These congressional guidelines do just that—provide specific limits to acceptable behavior.

Since the guidelines were issued, professional groups and publishers have met to discuss their impact on periodicals, specifically the limits imposed on interlibrary loan of periodicals. These guidelines (Commission on New Technological Uses of Copyrighted Works, or CONTU, Guidelines) will be discussed in the chapter on interlibrary loan. The following section will deal with local copying of books and periodicals.

Single Copies for Teachers

A teacher may copy (or ask to have copied) for the purposes of research, teaching, or preparation for teaching any of the following:

■ A single copy of a chapter from a book;

■ A single copy of an article from a periodical or newspaper;

■ A single copy of a short story, short essay, or short poem, even if it is contained in a collection;

■ A single copy of a chart, graph, diagram, drawing, cartoon, or picture from a book, periodical, or newspaper.

The teacher may retain the single copies of these materials in files for personal or research use or for use in teaching. This interpretation would permit reading the material to a class. A liberal, but not unjustifiable, interpretation of the guidelines would also allow the teacher to write the material on the blackboard or overhead projector for use in teaching.

The preceding permissions seem quite generous. The congressional guidelines, however, put some limits on these options. There are four significant prohibitions to the print permission, three of which have application to single copies for teachers:

■ Copying shall not be used to create or to replace or substitute for anthologies, compilations, or collective works. Such replace-

Q: We have a new poster-making machine. It will take an 8 1/2" X 11" copy or printout and make it into a 23" x 31" poster. If a teacher makes a photocopy of a page out of a textbook and uses the copy to make a poster for display in the classroom during the unit being taught, is it violating any copyright laws?

A: A single copy of something for personal research or *use in teaching* is permitted, so if the teacher *discards* the original photocopy and just keeps the poster, there should be a reasonable claim of fair use.

ment or substitution may occur whether copies of various works or excerpts therefrom are accumulated or reproduced and used separately. In other words, you can't create your own books by gathering bits and pieces from other sources. This would include notebooks of editorial cartoons, comic strips, series of essays, and the like.

■ There shall be no copying from works intended to be "consumable" in the course of study or of teaching. These include workbooks, exercises, standardized tests, test booklets, answer sheets, and similar consumable material.

■ Copying shall not substitute for the purchase of books, publishers' reprints, or periodicals; be directed by higher authority; or be repeated with respect to the same item by the same teacher from term to term.

The prohibitions are significant because they deal with guidelines often breached in daily school and library practice. A teacher may find an item in the library that seems relevant to a course. While copying some portion of the text is acceptable, copying more than the limited chapter, article, essay, or chart described in the law above would be considered to be substituting for the personal purchase of the work and would therefore be in violation of the congressional guidelines and of the copyright law itself. Financial loss to the copyright holder is the overriding consideration when a court is asked to consider a ruling of fair use, so anything beyond minimal copying would tend to tip the scales away from a justifiable claim of fair use.

Similarly, since copying may not be "directed by higher authority," an administrator, curriculum director, supervisor, or department head cannot direct a teacher or other staff member to copy copyrighted materials under fair use for whatever purpose. The copying must be initiated by an individual teacher for that teacher's use. An example of violation of this aspect of the law would be a principal telling a teacher to copy a specific article on an aspect of classroom management. The principal may ask the teacher to read the article but cannot order the copying of the article. The teacher may, however, decide to copy the article for files or for reading at a more convenient time. This decision originated with the teacher; hence there is no violation.

Another example of violation would be a department head directing teachers to copy the instructions from a set of standardized tests so that only one set of instructions will need to be purchased. Not only is this a violation of the prohibition on copy orders coming from a higher authority, it also is a direct attempt to deprive the copyright holder of sales, violating the fourth fair use factor: "the effect of the use upon the potential market for . . . the copyrighted work."

One very limited exception to this rule was granted by a modest revision to the law in 1996 that permits institutions serving the blind and physically handicapped to acquire or make adaptive copies in Braille or other formats (HR 3754, Public Law 104-197). The DMCA also allows an institution to make a digital archival copy of a work that cannot be replaced. The stopper to this provision is that the digital copy cannot be accessed from beyond the library walls. You may make the digital copy available only on the local network or on disc, not via the Internet.

Multiple Copies for Classroom Use

Multiple copying for classroom use is completely permissible, provided that certain tests are met. An instructor is prohibited from making more than one copy of the item for each student in the course, and each item copied must be used for classroom use or for discussion. Additionally, each copy must include a notice of copyright. (See Appendix D for form.) To clarify this point, if a teacher has 30 students, she may not make 45 copies assuming that some of the students will lose or mutilate their copies before the assignment is finished. The teacher must actually use the copies for a specific activity or discussion. She may not make the copies just to include them for their literary or cultural value, or as an optional supplement.

The requirement of notice of copyright is the most often neglected aspect of this section of the guidelines. Each copy must have a notice of the copyright holder. Ordinarily this can be as simple as a notation on the margin of the page such as "Copyright 1996, Big Publishing Co."

The three tests that each instance of copying must meet are brevity, spontaneity, and cumulative effect. These tests are very specific in nature, and each copy must meet all the criteria for each test. This wording is specified in the guidelines, so fudging on the limits is not a good idea.

Q: Is it okay for a teacher to record a picture book and let kindergarten students listen to the story on the tape while looking at the book?

A: There is a special exception to copyright law for handicapped users that allow this practice, but the person for whom you are recording the book must be blind or otherwise physically unable to use a book. The copy must also be made on a special recorder designed for handicapped users. Making a copy of a book by recording it is the same (according to the law) as making a copy by photocopying it. Remember that for picture books there is a copy limitation (under fair use) of two pages or 10 percent of the text, whichever is less.

Brevity

■ **Poetry:** If a poem is less than 250 words and is printed on not more than two pages, it may be copied in its entirety. If the poem is longer than 250 words, only 250 words may be copied. The law does allow an unfinished line to be included if the 250-word limit should happen to fall in the middle of a line.

■ **Prose:** If a complete article, story, or essay is less than 2,500 words, it may be copied in its entirety. For other types of prose, such as plays, novels, or letters, a copy must not be more than 1,000 words or 10 percent of the whole, whichever is less. No matter how short the work, one may legitimately copy an excerpt of 500 words. This means that if a work is only 1,000 words in total, a teacher may copy 500 words even though that amount exceeds the 10 percent guideline.

■ **Exception:** The type of literature, composed of text and significant illustrations, commonly called "picture books," is generally much shorter than the 2,500-word limit for complete copying. The law provides a specific prohibition against copying works of this type in their entirety (and it specifically includes similar works intended for adults, such as comic books). Only two pages of a picture book may be copied as long as those two pages do not comprise more than 10 percent of the text of the book.

- **Illustration:** One chart, graph, drawing, cartoon, diagram, or picture may be copied per book or periodical issue. These copies must be photocopies or other exact copies. Enlarging or modifying the illustration in any way violates the author's right of adaptation and display.

Spontaneity

The individual teacher must initiate the making of multiple copies. In other words, the department head cannot make copies to give to each teacher to use in class, nor can the principal copy copyrighted materials to hand out in certain classes. The law even goes so far as to state that the making of multiple copies must be at the inspiration of the individual teacher, implying that the department head or supervisor cannot even give the classroom teacher a list of appropriate items to be copied without violating the letter of the law. This doctrine is consistent with the prohibition of copying directed by a higher authority, as discussed earlier.

Q: Our tenth grade English teachers require their students to create an anthology of poetry, essays, short stories, and articles on one thematic aspect of the Holocaust. Since the law states that copying should not be used to create or be a substitute for anthologies, compilations, or collective works, is this a violation of copyright law?

A: The print anthologies restriction is addressed more to teachers who simply photocopy the work rather than purchase textbooks. If the students make only a single copy of the materials for their own projects, make the choice of what to copy, and the projects revert to the students at the end of the assignment, there should be no problem.

The rationale for the spontaneity rule is that the idea and decision to use the work and the moment it will be used for maximum teaching effectiveness are so close in time that it would be unreasonable to expect a timely reply to a request for permission. "Unreasonable" and "timely" are subject to some degree of latitude. How long should one expect to wait for permission to reproduce? Are two weeks enough? A month? A semester? As a rule of thumb, allow about three weeks for a reply. If teachers know at least three weeks ahead of time that they will need to copy something for use in class, they should write for permission. If they do not receive a reply in time, they could then proceed with the copying since there is not sufficient time to send a second query. Obviously, if an article, illustration, poem, or other printed matter comes to the attention of the teacher a matter of days before the time of optimum use, the teacher could make multiple copies for the class without writing for permission. The teacher may not, however, use that same article, illustration, or poem in subsequent semesters or years without permission.

Cumulative Effect

The last test that an instance of multiple copying must pass is that of cumulative effect. The guidelines want to assure that copying is not substituting for purchase of books and periodicals. Again, the law wants to protect authors and publishers by preserving the market for their materials. To comply with this test, the copying must be done for only one course. For example, a teacher may make copies of a poem for all freshman English classes (one copy per student), but may not copy the same poem for sophomore English classes.

The guidelines limit the number of copies that may be made from a single source or author during a school year (or a semester or quarter if this isn't a full-year class). A teacher may make class copies of one short poem, article, story, or essay or two excerpts from the same author during one term (year or semester or quarter). If the copies are taken from a collective work (a book of poetry or essays by multiple authors, for example), the teacher is limited to three or fewer items during a class term. She is also limited to three or fewer items copied from one periodical volume (not issue) during one term. Current news articles from newspapers and magazines are exempt from this requirement. When an item ceases to become "current news" is not defined, but a two-month window would be generous. While the above rules are very specific, you must also consider the four prohibitions to the print permission when determining fair use. (Three of them were quoted earlier).

1. Copying shall not be used to create or to replace or substitute for anthologies, compilations, or collective works. Such replacement or substitution may occur whether copies of various works or excerpts therefrom are accumulated or reproduced and used separately.

2. There shall be no copying from works intended to be "consumable" in the course of study or of teaching. These include workbooks, exercises, standardized tests, test booklets, answer sheets, and similar consumable material.

3. Copying shall not:

   - Substitute for the purchase of books, publishers' reprints, or periodicals;
   - Be directed by higher authority; or
   - Be repeated with respect to the same item by the same teacher from term to term.

4. No charge shall be made to the student beyond the actual cost of the photocopying.

   The intent of these prohibitions is to protect authors and publishers from teachers who would substitute copies for purchased books or workbooks.

Examples of Acceptable Multiple Copying:

- As a result of confusing reports about a nominee to the Supreme Court, a teacher requests the librarian to make 32 copies (one per student in his course) of a one-page, 475-word excerpt from a book. The students will use these for a written exercise in editorial writing. Each student's copy is free, and each copy includes a notice of copyright.

- An elementary teacher asks the clerical aide to make 19 copies (one per student) of a time line of the American Revolution. The students will include the diagram in a notebook they are creating to follow the events of the Revolution from beginning to end. Each copy includes notice of copyright.

- An English coordinator suggests that a particular poem might be good to teach the skill of identification of meter. The decision to use the poem is left up to the individual teacher.

■ Last year, a first grade teacher copied a word game out of a children's magazine for her students to use as they studied a specific letter sequence. This year she wants to use the same game. She plans in advance and writes for, and receives, permission.

Examples of Unacceptable Multiple Copying:

■ A teacher copies a column from five consecutive issues of a magazine, making a booklet of articles for each student in a class. This practice violates the prohibition against creating anthologies as well as the cumulative effect test against copying more than three articles from a periodical volume.

■ Every year an elementary teacher makes copies of the poem "There's a new kid on the block" to give to students on the day that a new student arrives in class. Using this poem every year violates the prohibition against copying the same item from term to term.

■ A teacher wishes to teach the concept of sequencing. To help students visualize the process, the teacher copies a short picture book for each student and then mixes up the pages. The students must put the book back into the correct sequence. This practice violates the limit on brevity in that only two pages or 10 percent may be copied from a picture book.

■ A debate teacher requests copies of several selected articles for students to use in preparing a defense. The copies cost $4.57 at a local copy shop. To make matters simpler, the teacher charges the students $5. The extra money goes into the fund used to buy ribbons for the debate tournament. This practice violates the fourth prohibition to multiple copies. The student may not be charged beyond the actual cost of the copies.

■ A principal reads an article appropriate to a staff development concept. She asks the secretary to make copies for all the teachers and place them in their mailboxes. This instance violates several regulations including "top-down" directives. Also, the teachers aren't students enrolled in a class. Copying for the purpose of staff development seldom gets a fair use exemption. It could be a fair use if the four factors of section 107 are met.

Anticipation of Requests

If a teacher knows that a particular item will be used year-to-year or term-to-term, the safest course is to write for permission. The same holds true if the teacher plans in September, for example, to use a particular poem at Thanksgiving. This gives her ample time to request permission from the copyright holder, likely the publisher. In such an instance, requesting and receiving permission are mandatory prior to copying, not optional.

In writing for permission, be sure to give a full citation of the material to be copied (author, title, edition), a description of the material to be copied (amount, page numbers, chapters), the number of copies to be made, how the material will be used, the method of distribution, charge (if any) for the materials, and the method of reproduction. (See Chapter 9 on permissions for a sample request.)

Check the back of the title page (or sometimes the introduction or acknowledgments) for the name of the copyright holder. If the holder is a publisher, the address can be found in *Books in Print*, *The Literary Marketplace*, or one of several directories of the publishing industry. If the copyright holder is an individual, the publisher may or may not be able to broker the permissions. Be especially alert to the fact that some materials appearing in copyrighted works are quoted with permission of the original copyright holder. Many books dealing with literary topics, such as literary criticism and literary collections and anthologies, will show lengthy copyright acknowledgements. Such items are usually acknowledged in a section on the same page as the copyright information or in a foreword or introduction. If any copies include this material, separate permission must be received from the copyright holders of those works.

Be aware that some copyright holders will attempt to abridge your rights under fair use. Their books and periodicals have a notice on the title page (or verso) that states, in some variation on these words, "This material may not be copied for any purpose." A more wordy version of the statement might read, "Infringement occurs when any part of the publication is reproduced to be distributed to anyone, within or outside of the subscriber's organization" (Hoart, n.d.). Neither of these statements is in conformance with the fair use guidelines. Even if such statements are published in the book or journal, any use meeting the requirements of fair use may be copied under that exemption. Don't let such statements intimidate you from using such material, provided your use complies with all the fair use provisions.

Consumable Materials

Consumable materials comprise much more than workbooks. The category includes workbooks, tests, standardized tests, coloring books, answer sheets, worksheets, cutouts, templates, and patterns intended to be destroyed in making the item. The prohibitions on multiple copying state that "there shall be no copying of or from materials intended to be consumable." Pattern books, such as knitting books or woodworking plans, probably don't qualify as consumable and would likely be afforded the protection of other printed works.

The problem is that there are multiple items in the teacher's bag of tricks that can be considered consumable yet are still copied, albeit illegally. Schools often draw on the "no-profit" defense when copying consumables, but such a defense doesn't take into consideration the other tests of fair use. All aspects of the fair use exemption must be considered when making copies. Here are some common examples of improper use of consumables:

■ A teacher buys a single copy of a book of worksheets and copies one of the worksheets for students to use when they have a substitute teacher.

■ A teacher buys a book of worksheets, then cuts the worksheets apart to create a new sheet, duplicating that new worksheet for the class.

- The new social studies books come with duplicator masters. The first year of use a teacher makes a set of worksheets for her class. The second year, the masters will not make readable copies, since the ink on the back of the master has been consumed. The teacher simply runs the master through the thermal copier to make a new master.

- A computer program provides a package of questionnaires on which to record responses to questions. These sheets may or may not be suitable for insertion into an automatic scoring machine. The publishing company sells replacement packages of the required questionnaires. When the supply of questionnaires runs low, the librarian photocopies a new supply from one of the originals, keeping an original on file to make future copies.

- A new math series comes with a package of standardized tests. In order to stretch a limited budget to buy a set of manipulatives, the school buys one package of the tests (enough for one classroom) and duplicates enough additional copies so all students in the grade level can take the test on the same day.

These uses (and infinite variations) are all out of compliance. But they would not be if the teacher had gotten permission from the publisher. Since publishers are in the business of selling consumable materials, it is unlikely they would grant blanket permission to reproduce their consumables. However, since printing their products involves materials and labor costs to them, they might be willing to work out a discount arrangement for a school to undertake the actual duplication of the material under a license agreement. It can't hurt to ask. The worst they can do is say no.

Periodicals

Copying periodical articles (including newspaper articles) falls into the same basket as copying most print materials. Periodical articles are mentioned specifically in the guidelines about single copies for teachers. An article from a periodical or newspaper is considered to be within limits of acceptable copying. In addition, copying a chart, graph, diagram, drawing, cartoon, or picture from a periodical or newspaper is also legal. Under the guidelines, current news articles are exempt from permission requirements; however, an item is "current" for only a short time. The three-week suggested time allowance for a response to a permission request is probably sufficient for this use, as well.

The guidelines on multiple copies for classroom use are much more specific with regard to types of acceptable copies, whether from books or periodicals. The guidelines for brevity apply equally to items copied from periodicals and newspapers.

Poetry taken from periodicals must meet the guidelines for poetry: If a poem is less than 250 words and is printed on not more than two pages, it may be copied in its entirety. If the poem is longer than 250 words, only 250 words may be copied. The law does allow an unfinished line to be included if the 250-word limit should happen to fall in the middle of a line.

Prose taken from periodicals must meet the test for prose: If a complete article, story, or essay is less than 2,500 words, it may be copied in its entirety. For other types of prose, a copy must not be more than 1,000 words or 10 percent of the whole, whichever is less, with a minimum acceptable copy limit of 500 words. In other words, if a work is only 1,000 words long, a teacher may copy 500 words even though that amount exceeds the 10 percent guideline.

Graphic material in periodicals may also be copied, provided the copying meets the test for illustrations: One chart, graph, drawing, cartoon, diagram, or picture may be copied per periodical issue. Beware of copying an item, a cartoon for example, from several issues of a periodical. The allowed limit is three per periodical volume. The number of issues making up a volume varies from periodical to periodical, but a volume is usually one year's publications.

The test of spontaneity is also applicable to copies from periodicals. The making of multiple copies must be at the "instance and inspiration" of the individual teacher. A supervisor may not direct a teacher to make multiple copies of material from any periodical. In addition, the decision to use the work and the time of its use in class must be so close that it would be unreasonable to expect a reply to a request for permission from a copyright holder. Again, the three-week window for permission appears to be adequate.

The guidelines also specify a test of "cumulative effect" to limit the number of instances of copying allowed. The "cumulative effect" guidelines affecting the copying of periodical materials are:

■ The copying must be done for only one course,

■ Only one entire article or two excerpts may be copied from the same author,

■ No more than three items from the same periodical volume may be copied during one class term (year or semester, depending on the course), and

■ No more than nine items may be copied in multiples per course during one class term.

Here are some examples of these rules applied to typical classroom uses of periodical copies:

■ The American history and government teacher finds an article applicable to both courses. She may not reproduce the article for both classes. She may post the original article on the class bulletin board, however, and ask students to read it there.

■ A biology teacher has already handed out two excerpts of works from Stephen Jay Gould for her class's study of evolution when she finds an even more enlightening article in the journal *Science*. She may not make multiple copies of the work without permission. She may, however, place her copy of the magazine on reserve in the library and require students to read it.

■ A third grade teacher has copied two different articles from this year's *Zoo Books* for her science class. In preparing a unit on poetry, she finds a poem in one of this year's issues. She may copy the poem, but no more items from that volume of the periodical for this term.

■ A sociology teacher uses magazines as a primary resource, copying articles to use as discussion starters and essay support. So far this term, he has copied eight articles to hand out to his classes. A new issue of *National Geographic* has two articles about primitive societies that he would like his students to compare and contrast. He may not copy both these articles since that would exceed the nine-items-per-term limitation.

Documents in the public domain, such as periodicals or monographs from the Department of Education or ERIC, do not count in the total copies per year as there is no restriction on duplication of public domain materials.

The general prohibitions on multiple copying apply to periodicals, also. Those prohibitions specify that copies may not be used to create or substitute for anthologies or compilations. The prohibitions state that the copies do not have to be "accumulated" to fall under this rule. "Accumulated," in this case, means collecting the copies and distributing them all at the same time, as if they were together in a booklet. The articles may be copied and used separately and still violate this prohibition.

Additionally, copying must not substitute for the purchase of a subscription to the periodical or publisher's reprints, it must not be ordered by a higher authority, and the same items may not be copied in succeeding class terms. Of course, the student may not be charged for the copies beyond the actual cost of the copies. The most significant consideration in this list is that of financial impact on the copyright owner. If the proposed fair use copying were to be repeated widely by many others, would such copying have an adverse effect on the copyright holder's revenues? If so, the use is undoubtedly not fair.

The lone exception to the rules on copying from periodicals is that of articles from current news periodicals (e.g. *Time*, *Newsweek*) and newspapers and the current news sections of other periodicals. According to the guidelines, copying such articles is in compliance. The only question would be how "current" the article is. While the guidelines do not define "currency," a window of two to four weeks would be appropriate and justifiable, especially around vacation periods when a new article may appear but the class will not meet for two weeks.

Copies for Vertical File

Q: *Can a library include in its vertical file magazine articles or pictures cut out of a magazine?*

A: As long as they are cut from the magazines, there is no problem. What is illegal is making copies and putting them in the vertical file.

Often a librarian will find an article in a magazine or newspaper that would be appropriate for inclusion in the vertical file. Perhaps the magazine title will be bound, and the librarian would like to avoid mutilating the bound copy to include the article in the vertical file. Such use is not within the scope of the library-permissible sections of the copyright law. However, if the library owns an item that is deteriorating or mutilated, lost or stolen, and a replacement cannot be obtained "at a fair price," the librarian may make a replacement copy of the damaged work. He may also make replacement pages for pages defaced or destroyed in materials the library already owns, but these copies are to replace the damaged sections of the magazines, not for the vertical file.

Additionally, a library may not retain photocopies of articles ordered for patrons through interlibrary loan. Photocopies for patrons are legal only when made for specific, individual users. Including such copies in the vertical file or a ready reference file would not be within the guidelines for such copying. Similarly, a librarian may not request copies of articles for library purposes, no matter how relevant the article might be to the library's patrons. Such ordering would deprive the publisher of a sale of an issue or a reprint and hence does not fall within the fair use exemption (Dukelow, p.36).

Copies for Reserve

Any library materials, or those of faculty members, may be put on reserve at any time. Such use has no impact on copyright at all. Making copies for reserve, however, enters into an entirely different arena. While there is no specific discussion of this procedure in the law, the American Library Association has written a model policy targeted to college and university libraries that takes into account various portions of the law that might impact copying for reserve. While the policy is targeted to college and university libraries, the extension of these guidelines to school libraries is not unreasonable.

The document Model Policy Concerning College and University Photocopying for Classroom Research and Library Reserve Use permits single copies of a book chapter, an entire periodical article, or a single poem. For multiple copies to fall within the policy, they must be

- Of a reasonable amount considering the nature of the course, its subject matter and level, and the amount of material usually assigned for a single class term;

- The number of copies should be less than six, unless six is not enough for enrollment in that course and others that can be anticipated to use the same material;

- Each copy must contain notice of copyright; and

- The effect of the copying should not diminish the market for the original. The policy strongly recommends that the library own a copy of the original (ALA, 1982, p.6).

Copies for Interlibrary Loan

The rules for interlibrary loan of periodicals are many and detailed. For a complete explanation of the regulations, see Chapter 8 on interlibrary loan, photocopying, facsimile, and document delivery.

Graphics

(**Note:** *This section will discuss the various acceptable uses of graphics from books and periodicals of many types. Posters, paintings, slides, and transparencies are covered in Chapter 4: Audiovisual Works.*)

Q: *I am putting up a Web page and want to post images of Cezanne and Van Gogh's paintings. If I take a photograph of a painting, can I use this?*

A: If you can get the museum to allow you to take a photo of the original (which is long out of copyright), you can post it. But, if you scan a professional photo of the old master painting, you have violated the copyright of the photographer (or more likely the museum, which owns the painting since it probably commissioned the photos.)

Q: *Photocopied pictures of scenes from movies are displayed on a bulletin board. Some pictures are from old movies while others are more recent. I didn't select the pictures, so I am not sure if more than one came from the same book. Is it a violation?*

A: If the bulletin board uses the teacher's own copies of these photos, there should be no problem. Remember that under fair use, anyone may make a single copy of something like a photo or chart for his personal research or teaching.

Graphics, including illustrations, graphs, diagrams, charts, drawings, cartoons, and pictures, are dealt with specifically in several sections of the copyright law and associated guidelines. The appeal of graphic representations to students makes schools especially vulnerable to infringement in this area.

The primary restriction to keep in mind when making decisions about copying graphics of any type is that the right to create "derivative works" rests with the copyright owner. In other words, while the guidelines give permission to make a copy or copies for educational purposes, those copies must be just that—exact copies. The right to change the chart, picture, cartoon, or illustration into a poster or slide or transparency or video or wall graphic (also called the right of adaptation) belongs to the copyright holder.

The rights to graphics sell for many thousands of dollars, and the owners of such copyrights vigorously defend their rights to control such use. Check any T-shirt or poster featuring a well-known cartoon character and you will see that the characters are copyrighted and usually trademarked as well. The owners of the rights to these characters would not have gone to the trouble to protect their works if they didn't intend to use all the resources of the law to guard their property. Discovery of a violation is usually announced with a letter from a law firm requesting the offenders "cease and desist" their suspected infringement. There are numerous stories of schools being cited for using blown-up Disney characters to decorate a building or classroom.

The most common type of violation in this area occurs via the opaque projector or overhead projector. Teachers will purchase a coloring book, greeting card, magazine illustration, cross-stitch pattern, or the like and enlarge it into a bulletin board decoration, wall graphic, poster, or big book. Even modification of the original will not protect them from liability. The Library of Congress Copyright Office's publication states: " . . . a copyrighted work would be infringed by reproducing it in whole or in any substantial part, and by duplicating it exactly or by imitation or simulation. Wide departures or variations from the copyrighted work would still be an infringement as long as the

Q: *A teacher has plastered his walls with newspaper cartoons. Is it a copyright violation for teachers to cut out cartoons and display them?*

A: Presuming that the teacher bought the book or newspaper, she may cut it up and post the cartoons on her wall. The teacher may also make a single copy of a cartoon for her personal use for teaching.

author's 'expression' rather than merely the author's 'ideas' [is] taken" (Copyright Office, p.8). A colleague once justified massive copies of Disney characters by making one slight modification to each character. The characters were instantly recognizable, however, and would have merited at least a cease-and-desist order had they been discovered.

Graphic artists are in the business of selling their artistic expressions. Garfield, Snoopy, Spiderman, Bugs Bunny, the Disney characters, and others are all highly protected by legions of aggressive attorneys. Virtually all of these characters have been used extensively in educational materials and bulletin board decorations. By adapting the characters for specific classroom use, a teacher deprives the creator of potential sales of that character and usurps the right of the copyright holder to decide how the creation will be used. While it is possible to write for permission to reproduce such graphic characters, permission is seldom granted. A better suggestion would be to write to the franchise-holding company and request they produce the type of material the teacher is seeking.

Teacher-created graphics are always safe as long as they are truly teacher-created and not just hand-drawn copies of copyrighted professional materials. In addition, some books of bulletin board ideas give permission to enlarge and adapt the material within. Naturally, those items are already copyright-clear. There are some books of public domain art that may be freely copied, enlarged, and adapted, and those are a good source of decorations.

Music

Making copies of print music involves some special guidelines. In 1976, at the same time Congress was developing the Fair Use Guidelines, several music industry groups and music educators developed the Guidelines for Educational Uses of Music. The groups participating included Music Publishers' Association of the United States, Inc., the National Music Publishers' Association, Inc., the National Music Teachers Association, the Music Educators National Conference, the National Association of Schools of Music, and the Ad Hoc Committee on Copyright Law Revision. Since these guidelines aren't law, they are more of a "gentlemen's agreement" that the uses described are acceptable by all parties. The primary groups who would potentially sue a school are included, so staying within these guidelines is a sensible fair practice. You might be able to make a case for slight extensions of the limits detailed here, but just as in speeding, the more you exceed the limits the more you risk a penalty. As in all the fair use guidelines, if the proposed use exceeds the guidelines, you may always fall back on the four-pronged fair use analysis to determine if your use might be fair.

Some examples of acceptable copying of printed music are:

■ Emergency copying when purchased copies have not arrived in time for a performance, with the understanding that the emergency copies will be replaced with the purchased copies.

■ For nonperformance classroom purposes, you may make one or more copies of portions of works, as long as the copies do not constitute a "performable unit such as a section, movement or aria." The copied portion may not exceed 10 percent of the whole work. Only one copy per pupil is permitted.

■ If the school buys printed music, you may edit or simplify those copies as long as you don't change the fundamental character of the work (e.g. jazz stays jazz) or alter or add lyrics (if none exist).

■ You may make a single copy of recordings of performances by students but it may only be used for evaluation or rehearsal. Either the teacher or the school may keep this recording.

■ You may make a single copy of a sound recording of copyrighted music (as long as a teacher or the school owns the recording) for the purpose of constructing "aural exercises or examinations." The teacher or the school may keep this derivative recording. (This permission pertains only to the copyright of the printed music and not to any copyright that may exist in the sound recording.)

The guidelines prohibit several types of music copying:

■ Any copying that substitutes for purchasing a collection, anthology, or collection of music.

■ Any copying of "consumable" materials such as workbooks, tests, or exercises.

■ Copying music for performance, except as explained in the first permission above.

■ Copying with the intention of not purchasing music, except as explained in the first and second permissions above.

■ Copying without including of the copyright notice that appears on the printed copy.

Q: The music appreciation class wants to take portions of recordings and make "listening tests." Since this is an anthology, is this permitted?

A: According to the guidelines for Educational Uses of Music, taking excerpts of school-owned recordings for "aural examinations" is permitted.

Q: Our high school recently staged a musical and legitimately purchased the production rights for this event. A parent videotaped the performance and now would like to make copies of the videotape to sell to parents of cast members at exactly the cost of making the copies. These tapes would be used only for the enjoyment of the students' families. Will this violate copyright law?

A: Unless the school (or the parent) also purchased rights to distribute the production, this would likely be a violation of copyright The law doesn't address this specific situation but it does address performances of music. A school may make a single tape of a musical performance, but that copy can be used only in class to critique the performance.

Glossary

Accumulation: Gathering together reproductions to be distributed at one time. Accumulated copies do not count as one; they count as the total of the parts. Also, copies do not have to be distributed at once to be considered an anthology.

Collective work: A work written by two or more authors, each of whom contributes separate, identified portions of the work.

Current news: Descriptions of events that have happened in the recent past. Some magazines and newspapers contain nothing but current news, while others mix current news with commentary, essays, and personality pieces. Only current news is offered a special exemption from copy limits.

Notice of copyright: Required notice on fair use reproductions of copyrighted material. The notice must include the name of the copyright holder and the date of copyright, such as "Copyright 1997, Linworth Publishing." The notice must appear on each copy.

Periodical volume: The binding increment of a periodical. Most periodicals assemble volumes based on a 12-month period (though the year may start in January, July, or any other month), but others use a two-volume-per-calendar-year arrangement.

Term: The length of time to complete a course. An English class might span an entire school year, while an elective class such as psychology might meet for only a semester or quarter. The term of the English class is a year, while the term for the elective is either a semester or quarter. One must consider the term of the course when evaluating the ability to reproduce materials for that course.

Chapter *4*

Audiovisual Works

T he law defines "audiovisual" as follows:

> *"Audiovisual works" are works that consist of a series of related images which are intrinsically intended to be shown by the use of machines, or devices such as projectors, viewers, or electronic equipment, together with accompanying sounds, if any, regardless of the nature of the material objects, such as films or tapes, in which the works are embodied.*

Guidelines for use of audiovisual works vary widely. Depending on the medium and the method of acquisition, rights may vary from unlimited to short-lived. The Copyright Act of 1976 was written, in part, to address the needs of producers of audiovisual materials who were concerned that their property was not being adequately protected under the old law. The new law clarified many ambiguities, though often not in favor of educators.

The same fair use guidelines that apply to print materials do not apply to audiovisuals. Because of the nature of the audiovisual medium, producers worry not only about unauthorized copies but also about losing profits from unauthorized performances of the protected works. Producers of music recordings, movies, and television programs make their money from licensing those works for public exhibition and broadcast as well as from direct sales, so they are especially wary about what end users will do with the copy they have purchased. Had Congress allowed as free rein for copying audiovisuals as they permitted for print materials, these media producers feared they would be cheated of profits that were rightfully theirs.

Aside from playwrights, copyright owners of print materials needn't worry much about their performance rights because performance of print materials is not much of a problem. The right of adaptation is reserved for the copyright holder in all circumstances, and mounting a performance of a print work is no simple feat. In order for a print work to be "performed," it must be adapted for a play or painting or sound recording—a straightforward violation of copyright. But if graphic or illustrative materials are involved, a "performance" is as simple as a display. Simply tacking up a copyrighted work, when not associated with an educational fair use exemption, would be a technical violation of copyright if the display were intended for others to view.

What Is a Public Performance?

Q: Our school will charter large, commercial buses for an extended field trip. The buses have VCRs and TVs. We would like to show a tape of a movie owned by one of the teachers to keep the children occupied while we make this lengthy trip. Is this legal?

A: Probably not unless performance rights were acquired with the tape. This use of video is not face-to-face instruction. It probably involves some people who are not students and teachers in the class, such as a bus driver or chaperones, and the bus might be considered a bit strange for an instructional locale. The copyright holder, however, could grant (or sell) you one-time public performance rights.

Virtually any copyrighted work—music, drama, dance, motion picture, literary work, or other audiovisual expression—may be performed publicly. A public performance need not be a gala event in an auditorium. Something as seemingly trivial as popping a cassette into a boom box can be classed as a public performance, given the proper circumstances. Those circumstances are clearly defined in the law: "A place open to the public or at any place where a substantial number of persons outside of a normal circle of a family or its social acquaintances is gathered. . ."

Any display or performance of a copyrighted work under these circumstances would require a license. The gray area of this definition is the "substantial number." How many people outside the normal circle of a family does it take to cross the line into public performance? Unfortunately, the law and the fair use guidelines don't quantify this number. Court precedent doesn't give much guidance, either. However, a major movie studio did attempt to sue a woman who showed one of the studio's movies to the guests at her child's birthday party saying that this event exceeded the exemption afforded a family and its social acquaintances. Alas, the movie studio dropped the suit because of extensive unfavorable publicity before a court could make a determination of the number of "friends" it takes to cross the line into public performance.

Under normal conditions, a classroom full of students and teachers would meet the criteria for public performance, since they would constitute a group "outside of a normal circle of a family or its social acquaintances." Hence, displaying a film or playing a tape to a classful of students could constitute a public performance and would therefore require a license or other permission.

Fair Use of Audiovisual Materials

Q: My question is not for curriculum-related showing but for the days that teachers use videos for nothing but babysitting or "rewards." In that case isn't it a violation to air a "home-use only" tape from Blockbuster if the purpose is entertainment?

A: It makes no difference *where* the tape is from, for either curricular or reward showings. The only significant concern is whether you have public performance rights for the tape. Blockbuster doesn't sell or rent public performance rights; hence you can use the tapes in only curricular situations. If your library owns the tape, for instance, and you have public performance rights with the tape, you can show it for whatever purpose you want. If you don't own performance rights, however, you can legally show it only in curricular situations.

The law does provide a type of "fair use" exemption for performance or display of a work in schools, however. Four requirements must be met before a performance is considered acceptable under this educational exemption to the public performance restriction:

1. The performance must be presented by instructors or pupils,

2. The performance must occur in the course of face-to-face teaching activities, and

3. The performance must take place in a classroom or similar place of instruction (including the library) in a nonprofit educational institution; and

4. The performance must be of a legally acquired (or legally copied) copy of the work. (The presenter is protected from liability for illegal copies *if* the presenter is unaware that the copies were not legally acquired or made.)

Note that all four of these conditions must be met before a performance is considered exempt from the public performance requirements. If these four factors were rephrased into a yes-no test, a "no" response to any one of these questions would indicate that the performance is not permitted under the fair use provision of the law.

In understanding each of the four factors, some ground rules must be established. In factor one, "instructors" and "pupils" are those teachers and pupils enrolled in that particular class. Visitors to the class, parents who happen to drop in, vendors or publishers' representatives, PTA officers, or other students not enrolled in this class would make the mix of viewers broader than the pupil and teacher restriction.

The "face-to-face teaching" restriction has been variously interpreted to mean that only if the teacher and the student are in the same room at the same time can a showing be held to be protected under fair use. While this is a valid criterion, other factors come into play in this issue. "Face-to-face" also requires that the showing be directly related to the curriculum. In other words, the display of the work must be related to the lesson at hand, not simply related to some type of lesson past or a lesson to come.

For example, the freshman English curriculum might require the students to read Shakespeare's *Romeo and Juliet* in September each year. However, the English teacher needs some time to prepare final exams later in the semester, so she decides to show the Franco Zefferelli film of the play to occupy her students while she works on the exam months after the class has studied the play. Such use of the video would probably not be within the fair use exemption since the class is no longer studying the play. A good rule of thumb to determine if use of a video is acceptable is to ask, "Is this an integral part of the unit I am teaching right now?" If the answer is "no," then the showing is probably a public performance. Beware of loose or questionable links from audiovisual material to lessons. Showing *Babe* because the class has been studying the farm is not a reasonable tie-in unless your local farms have talking animals. The same rationale would apply to showing *The Lion King* during a study of Africa or the great cats. There are many more curriculum-appropriate materials you could select.

Classroom- or school-wide use of audiovisuals for entertainment or reward is specifically prohibited under fair use. Many teachers and schools use showings of popular movies to reward attendance, good behavior, or academic performance. These showings may take place in an instructional place, may be performed by teachers for students, and the copy of the program may be legally acquired, but reward or entertainment is not considered "face-to-face" teaching, regardless of the virtue of perfect attendance, exemplary behavior, or high test scores. Unless a specific teaching goal is documented in a district curriculum guide or state standard, one may reliably count on the need for a performance license.

Several vendors sell so-called "umbrella licenses" that permit the school or library to show noncurricular films and videos from limited lists of producers. There are pros and cons to these licenses. A library-only license makes the librarian (and the library) the local "babysitter." Whenever the PE teacher is out, the kids are sent to the library to see movies to keep them entertained. If you have a building-wide license, teachers become lax in their use of video. The primary vendor of these licenses is Movie Licensing USA. See the Appendix for contact information.

Additionally, beware of what might be called "general cultural value." Certainly there are many wonderfully educational videos on the market and perhaps in your library or personal video collection. However, showing these types of videos to a class without a specific curricular objective is not permitted under the "face-to-face" rule. If the objective isn't specified in the curriculum guide for this particular class, showing a video on that topic is a public performance, and license or permission is required.

Keep in mind that what is "curricular" for one class might not be part of the curriculum for another, no matter how "educational" the topic might be. For example, a French class might be able to show the movie *The Red Balloon* as an example of French culture (part of the curriculum for that class), while an English class would have difficulty tying in this wordless film to its literature objectives.

You need also to take the location of the performance into account when calculating fair use. Showings in a classroom are certainly acceptable, as are showings in auditoriums, gymnasiums, libraries, and other typical instructional places. Some would like to stretch "instructional place" to include school buses, churches, or other nonstandard locations. One must weigh those performances carefully. The odder the location, the stronger your rationale should be for the other three requirements for a fair use performance.

When you consider if the item to be performed is legally acquired, you really must ask if it has been paid for. If you purchase the tape or disc (either at school or at home), you have legally acquired it. If you borrow a copy from a library or a friend who has purchased that copy, it has been legally acquired. If you rent a video or compact disc from a video store, the store purchased that copy of the item, so it has been legally acquired.

There is one exception to the "paid for" rule of thumb. Videos taped off the air following the Off-air Taping Guidelines are considered to be legally acquired when shown within the retention time limits. There is a legal loophole that says an end-user who is caught with an illegal disc or tape is not liable for copyright infringement if he had no knowledge that the item was illegally acquired. This loophole is really meant to protect those people who buy "pirated" items unknowingly, not to provide an escape for those who decide to retain off-air videos beyond the erase date.

Q: Several teachers teaching the same subject want to view a video program at the same time. I am asked to show the video in a distribution system that would make it available, not just to these five teachers but to every teacher in the building. Is it legal for me to do this?

A: It is legal for you to show this video to the five teachers whose curriculum pertains to the video. You can even do that through a video distribution system. Other classes watching the same video, however, (those whose current curriculum does *not* include the topic of the video) would not be compliant showings.

New Technologies Pose New Questions

Teachers often ask questions about out-of-the-ordinary performances of audiovisual materials. As new technologies have proliferated in schools, interpretations of copyright fair use guidelines have become stretched. Closed-circuit television systems, video distribution systems, and just cabling two televisions together to accommodate large audiences weren't foremost in the minds of legislators when the guidelines were written. Closed-circuit television systems (nonpublic broadcasts between school campuses) have been held to require special licensing. According to the late Ivan Bender, former attorney for the Association for Information Media and Equipment (AIME), an industry-sponsored copyright enforcement group, the term "face-to-face" simply implies that the information may not be transmitted into the classroom unless that transmission format serves only to link classrooms that receive that particular program, i.e., an in-house video distribution system (Bender, p. 54). So hooking two televisions together would be acceptable, as would using one of the many in-house distribution systems, as long as only the students enrolled in the class see or hear the program. Nonstandard campus arrangements (e.g. a high school and a middle school on the same campus) will require serious investigation to determine if they meet the single-campus requirement. In making the determination, consider if there are two or more administrative units in the building. Even if there is only one library between the two units, the fact that there are two principals or administrators would seem to point to two separate campuses for licensing purposes.

It is imperative that presenters read labels on audiovisual materials because restrictions printed thereon (aside from "home use only" labels) are binding, subject to licensing or other written permission. Innocent infringement (violation of the law because of lack of knowledge that a particular use would be noncompliant) is difficult to claim when the producer clearly states on the label that public performances are not permitted. Items with homemade labels should be viewed with a jaundiced eye as they are likely to be either illegally copied or subject to additional restrictions based on format or method of reproduction (e.g., off-air tapes.)

Under the preceding regulations, the following are examples of acceptable and unacceptable performances:

Q: Is it a violation of copyright to show just a clip of a movie?

A: As long as the clip doesn't constitute the "essence" of the work (that is convey the whole point of the film in that scene or clip– like the final scene in *Bonnie & Clyde*) you should be okay. Remember, you can't put that clip on another tape. You *must* run it from a full copy of the video.

Examples of Acceptable Performances:

■ A teacher shows a library-owned filmstrip to his sixth-grade science class to demonstrate the effects of water pollution as part of a lesson on ecology. This use is protected under the educational exemption because it meets all of the above criteria: It is presented for enrolled students by an instructor in face-to-face teaching in a classroom; the copy is legally owned by the library (or at least the teacher has no reason to think it is not legally acquired.)

■ An English teacher's classes have been studying *Romeo and Juliet*. To conclude the unit, the teacher shows the English Department's tape of the Franco Zefferelli version of the play in class, spreading the program over three class days. This use is also protected under the educational exemption. The teacher is showing the program; it is an integral portion of the lesson; the performance is taking place in the classroom; and the copy has been purchased by the English Department.

■ An elementary school music teacher plays a recording of a performance of John Philip Sousa's "Stars and Stripes Forever" as part of a unit on patriotic music for third graders. The recording accompanied the music text. While the medium has changed, the guidelines remain the same. This is a performance in class, by a teacher, within a lesson plan, with a legally acquired copy.

Examples of Unacceptable Performances

■ The PTA shows a library-owned copy of The Little Mermaid to the children of members in a classroom while the officers have a meeting in the library. The copy is legally acquired, the performance takes place in a classroom, and the performance may be presented by a teacher or pupil, but this performance is not a part of face-to-face teaching activities. This would be considered entertainment or reward, and as such is not permitted without public performance rights. This example would require payment of royalties for the performance. Renting a copy of the video would have no effect on the legality of the performance, and the school may be liable for providing equipment for an infringing performance. The same prohibition would apply to movies or recordings used to reward classes for good grades, commendable behavior, or perfect attendance.

■ On the last day of the semester, the American history teacher decides to play for his class a record on the Cuban missile crisis so he can calculate grades while the students are occupied. The class is not currently studying that portion of the curriculum. This use is not acceptable because the face-to-face teaching requirement is not met. While a weak case can be made for the fact that the topic will eventually be covered, this topic is not under the current lesson plan. Public performance rights would be recommended in this case.

■ Because the drama teacher gives such hard tests, a group of drama students decides to rent a video of a play they have been studying and show it in the drama room after school to review for the upcoming exam. Several of the students plan to bring friends to watch the movie with them. This would definitely be considered a public performance because nonstudents (the friends) are involved in the session. This would also not be considered face-to-face teaching because the instructor did not participate in the meeting.

The key to using audiovisual materials in a school setting lies in meeting all four tests of acceptable use:

■ Face-to-face teaching,

■ Presented by teachers or pupils,

■ In a classroom or similar setting of a nonprofit educational institution,

■ With a legal copy of the work.

Since many audiovisual materials may be purchased with public performance rights, wise librarians track which of their materials have such rights, using entries in the shelf list or catalog, stickers on individual items, or log books to mark the items for which rights have been purchased. A notation on how the rights were acquired and how long they will last would be helpful, e.g., "via catalog," "life-of-tape," or "on P.O. #123456, 2 years (exp. 11-15-99)."

A file of performance rights documentation is also a good idea. A few suppliers, especially video producers, provide blanket public performance rights in the prices of all videos in their catalogs. A photocopy of this statement from the catalog attached to the purchase order for the videos should be sufficient documentation. Another supplier includes a statement on the order envelope stating, "The video cassettes you purchase from XYZ Company are sold for school and library use. Broadcast rights are not included. Programs may not be reproduced, copied, or transmitted without written permission." An extra-clear method of stating the conditions of your purchase would be to include a line on the purchase order stating, "All materials to include public performance rights" (or archival rights). Acceptance of the order with this statement on it would contractually oblige the supplier to provide public performance rights as well. (Figure 4.1)

Caveat: **Be certain that you are sending the order to a company that is able to broker such licenses. Some AV jobbers will supply the tapes on the purchase order even though they are not able to broker the performance rights.**

The sale of public performance rights is a contractual obligation, so the purchaser and the copyright owner (usually through a supplier or distributor) can negotiate whatever rights package the owner would like to sell and the purchaser can afford. Don't be afraid to propose the type of performance rights you need. The worst the copyright owner can do is say no. Just make sure you prepare your proposal far in advance of your anticipated performance date. There is no "fair use" on public performances, and if you have not acquired the necessary rights before your public performance, you are on extremely hazardous ground.

Figure 4.1   *Sample Purchase Order*

Purchase Order #12345123
Smallville Independent School District
4321 S. Front Street
Middletown, USA

To: Video Supplier
    1234 Main Street
    Hollywood, CA

Please accept our order of the following:

Quanity	Title	Price
1	Copyright and You (VHS)	25.00
1	A school librarian's view of copyright (VHS)	50.00
	Shipping	5.00
Note: All videos will include public performance rights. If additional charges are required, confirmation must be received before shipment.		
	TOTAL	$80.00

Archiving Audiovisual Works

Copyright law pertaining to computer software allows the purchaser to make a single backup copy (also called archival copy) of the diskettes in case something happens to the original diskettes. Unfortunately, audiovisual materials do not offer the same archival permission as does computer software. Owners of film, video, or audio may not make backup copies of the works. The usual terms of purchase are similar to that of a book: You may use the material until it wears out or breaks. At that point you may attempt to repair it, but the best alternative is to replace the work. In the case of video and audio, this is called "life of tape." You have the right to use the program as long as the tape works. When the tape wears out, it is time to buy a replacement. The good news is that tape costs are usually quite reasonable, at least for works available from more than one source.

> *Q:* I have some very expensive videos in my library collection and I'm afraid to circulate them for fear that something might happen to them. May I make an archival copy of the video as I do the computer diskettes we circulate?
>
> *A:* No, you can't without specific permission to do so. Copyright laws give express permission to make archival copies of computer software only. No other medium is granted such permission. However, if the video is on Beta tape (now obsolete) the DMCA allows you to transfer the tape to a current technology (VHS or digital)

When a film breaks, since backup onto tape is not permitted (as this would be change of format), the only alternatives consistent with copyright law are to splice the film or to purchase replacement footage if the damage is extensive. The same holds true with audiotape. Backups onto other tapes or digital media (compact disk or digital audio storage) are not allowed. This prohibition is waived when a copyrighted work is recorded on a medium that is no longer in popular use, such as Beta format videotape. Because Beta format is obsolete, you may transfer your Beta programs onto VHS tape or digital storage without specific permission for each program. The DMCA defines "obsolete" thus: "[T]he machine or device necessary to render perceptible a work stored in that format is no longer manufactured or is no longer reasonably available in the commercial marketplace."

For graphic material, you may make efforts to preserve the material by framing, encapsulating, or laminating, but you may not archive or reproduce that material using color copiers, scanners, or other image-making technology.

Sound Recordings

Sound recordings, as used in this section, will include phonograph records, cassette tapes in analog and digital formats, compact discs, reel-to-reel tape, and hard disk-based recordings. All these formats can be and are copyrighted. Even if you do not see a copyright symbol on the item itself, because the law no longer requires notice of copyright, you must assume all materials to be copyrighted unless specifically shown otherwise. Some recordings use the special symbol assigned to phonorecords—a 'p' in a circle, similar to the 'c' in a circle that means "copyrighted."

A: Not only is this making an anthology, it is reproduction (a protected right) and distribution (yet another protected right). None of these suggested uses says anything about curriculum, classroom teaching, or any of the other triggers that might bring in a discussion of fair use. Of course, at the scope suggested, fair use would likely be out the window anyway.

Playing the original recordings in the classroom, as long as they are

- Directly tied to the lesson at hand in that specific classroom at the time, *and*
- The teacher is the one to make the decision to use the tapes (Remember— a bottom-up copying scheme),*and*
- The only ones to hear the tape are the students and teachers in the class, *and*
- You are in a nonprofit educational institution, *and*
- You are working with a legally acquired (i.e. bought) copy of the work, you should be okay. The problem here is that under the AV guidelines (basically summarized above) you must comply with *all* of the provisions. If you say no to any of the conditions, you don't qualify for fair use.

When a sound recording is played publicly, the composer of the music is entitled to a royalty, but the performer of the music is not. The performers do receive royalties from sales of recordings, but not from public performances. The reasoning here is that sound recordings do not have public performance rights. However, jazz recordings, and some blues recordings, are performances covered by copyright because these styles of music rely heavily on improvisation. Since the work is "fixed" only at the time of recording, there is a dual copyright—that of the composer who wrote the melody and that of the performer who improvised on it. Since the Internet has become an active medium in the transmission of sound recordings, and because many people are copying CDs and tapes from the Internet rather than buying them, Congress in 1995 granted public performance rights to "digital audio performances." Web pages that deliver recordings on the request of the viewer may be in violation of this revision to the law (Section 114(d-f).

Sound recordings have the same requirements and permissions as do all audiovisual materials. See Chapter 4 (page 45) on the four tests of fair use for the specific details. Sound recordings of music add an extra onus to the mix. A work may involve three copyrights: one for the music itself, a second for the recording, and a third on the arrangement. For example, a current hit record may have music and lyrics copyrighted by the author, while the actual recording of the performance of that music and lyrics may be covered by an entirely different copyright. In order to receive permission to use the recording in any derivative work, videotape, or public performance, you must get permission from all copyright holders.

Occasionally a teacher will ask students to perform music and record the performance to use as background music for a multimedia presentation. Even if the music is in the public domain, the arrangement of the music may not be. Additionally, the students now own the copyright to their own performance of the music. Clearance will be required for any use beyond that by the students involved.

Two organizations do most of the copyright clearances for professional music recordings: American Society of Composers, Authors and Publishers (ASCAP) and Broadcast Music Inc. (BMI). You can contact these organizations at

ASCAP
One Lincoln Plaza
New York, NY 10023
212/621-6000
or on the Internet at <www.ascap.com>.

BMI
320 W. 57th St.
New York, NY 10019
212/586-2000
or on the Internet at <www.bmi.com>.

As with all audiovisual materials, the owner of a sound recording is not permitted to make any copies of the original, even archival copies. Some tapes may be purchased with duplication rights, especially foreign language tapes. Be sure to retain the paperwork granting the duplication rights and any restrictions that may accompany them, e.g., duplication of one copy per student or one copy per textbook purchased. If such numerical restrictions apply, create and maintain a log of duplications (Figures 4.2 and 4.3). bit of extra time spent in the process can save many hours of research compiling records at a later date, should you be challenged on compliance.

Sampling. The amazing capabilities of digital editing equipment make all sorts of creative work with audio not only possible but simple. This equipment is so sophisticated that individual wave forms can be edited, copied, modified, or erased. The technology is called "sampling." Several lawsuits have been filed and won against people who extracted selected sounds from a copyrighted work and inserted them into a new, derivative work. How were they caught? Does it make any difference? They were caught, found guilty in an expensive trial, and paid the penalties. But if you need ammunition to convince crafty audiophiles, there are certain digital "signatures" that enable audio to be quite simply identified (with the necessary equipment and expertise).

Sampling tips:

Sample from your own recordings (ones you or your students recorded.) You will still need permission from music publishers if you are sampling from recorded music rather than voices or environmental sounds, but you will have one less permission to seek.

Remember (and remind students and colleagues) that there is a difference between "can" and "supposed to." You can sample from virtually any audio source. You are not supposed to do so without permission.

Q: *A teacher is teaching a unit on science fiction. She would like to use short clips from several science fiction movies. Can this be handled in a legal manner?*

A: The answer is "It depends." If she has the clips cued up on the tapes, and she punches play, runs the clips, then pops out the tape and does the same to the next one, sure. If she wants to make a new tape with just the clips in question, the answer is *no.* That is considered making an anthology and is not permitted. *However,* if she will make a multimedia program such as PowerPoint she can use up to three-minute clips of video in that presentation, but she will need to check the new multimedia guidelines for the specific limits, retention times, and re-use limits.

Figure 4.2 *Sample Duplication Log*

Audio Tape Duplication Log

Date	Tape	Copies	Comments
7/22	Un jour en France	15	Dubonet– 235 remain
8/15	Un jour en France	10	Martin– 225 remain
8/16	Habla espanol	13	Spanish 4 1/student

Figure 4.3

Audio Tape Duplication Log

Date	Tape	Copies	Comments

Film and Video

Unless you plan to use videocassettes as doorstops, using a film or video in a school necessarily involves a display or "performance" of the work. The right of public display is reserved for the copyright holder, as established in the law, but certain use of copyrighted films and videos is granted under the educational exemption to this part of the statute. In order for a school to use a film or video in the educational program without having to pay royalties for public performance, the use must meet all four of the following criteria:

■ The performance must take place in a classroom or other place of instruction in a nonprofit educational institution; and

■ The performance must be directed by students or teachers of the institution; and

■ The performance must be in the course of face-to-face teaching activities; and

■ The performance must be made from a copy of the work, which was legally made or acquired.

Note that all of the four criteria must be met in order for the showing to be exempt from the copyright holder's right of performance or display. The lack of compliance with even one of the four guidelines means public performance rights are required.

The means of acquisition of the video or film is not important (assuming it is legal) for compliant educational use. Rental videos and films may be used in the same manner as copies owned by the school, library, or school district. Copies owned by individual faculty members or students' families may also be used, as long as the copies were legally acquired. While the librarian needn't demand receipts from students and teachers, a cautious approach would dictate that outside videos be accompanied by a statement from the owner verifying ownership (Figure 4.4). Should the copy later be determined to be fraudulent, the school and library then have a solid case that they had no knowledge that the tape was in violation.

Of course, common sense would tell you that if the tape is not in a standard commercial case or is obviously re-taped, the program is probably not legally acquired. In such a case, the librarian would be wise to refuse to show such a program, or to provide equipment to do so. A school or district policy addressing videos not owned by the school is an essential part of effective copyright compliance. The policy should be approved by the

Q: The orchestra director would like to have a concert using movie theme songs. We would like to play a video of the movie while the orchestra is playing. Our question is how can we use the video without breaking any copyright laws?

A: This isn't face-to-face instruction, and simply answering "no" to that qualifying question means that you don't qualify for an automatic fair use exemption. You can, however, go through the four tests of fair use to see if you qualify on those grounds.

Q: Administrators ask the library staff to put videos from the library collection in the media distribution system so students can view them on two large-screen TVs in the cafeteria during the five lunch periods. Isn't this in violation of copyright law on public performance?

A: This is likely a violation. You may, however, show videos for which you own public performance rights.

board, supported by the principal, and annually called to the attention of the faculty. Such a policy would give the librarian a firm foundation to deny a faculty member's request to use questionable material.

Home Use Only

Many videos have a "home use only" sticker on the case. Some libraries and schools are fearful that they are taking a risk when they use tapes so labeled. The truth is that simply placing a "home use only" sticker on a video does not restrict a school from lending a copy owned by the library or using the program if the use otherwise meets all of the four criteria set forth above.

Once a tape has been sold, the "right of first sale" states that the copyright owner's exclusive distribution right to that copy has ceased (Reed, p. 2). The transfer of the right of distribution is the essential transaction that allows libraries to lend books and other materials. Note that only the right of distribution has ceased. The right of performance and display still resides with the copyright owner. In other words, the purchaser of a film or video may lend, sell, or give the copy to whomever she wishes without worry. Performances of the film or tape, however, must still comply with the law regarding performances or displays.

Caution: Watch carefully for producers or suppliers who sell you a license to a program rather than the program itself. Licensing a program is a way for a copyright owner to retain the distribution right since there is no actual sale. If you purchase a license to a program, you will be subject to any restrictions the copyright owner may choose to impose, including restricting your right to lend the program.

Mary Hutchings Reed, consultant to the American Library Association, recommends that "home use only" labels be allowed to remain on videos owned by a library (Reed, p. 2). A library would not want to appear to encourage copyright infringement, lest it be considered a contributory or vicarious lawbreaker. The "home use only" label will remind patrons that the video is not licensed for public performance, and while any lawfully acquired film or video may be used in a qualifying educational setting, these videos are still subject to copyright restrictions in the matter of public performance. The following practices are never acceptable with film or video:

- Making an anthology or collection from clips or excerpts;

- Transferring the work to another medium, e.g., film to video, or video to computer disk except in cases of obsolete media; or

- Using a program for recreation or reward without acquiring performance rights.

Off-Air Recording

To the average classroom teacher, a videotape is a videotape; you stuff it into a recorder and press "Play." But to the librarian who must sort through the jumble of copyright, a teacher approaching with a videotape in hand may be as welcome as a visit from a werewolf. A video of unknown origin is about as dangerous.

Q: I missed taping a television program that one of my teachers requested. May I ask a librarian at another school to make a copy of her tape for us?

A: No. Even if the producer of the television program offers taping rights to educators, you are granted the right only to tape the program directly off the air. Making copies within your own institution is permitted only if you need more than one copy for multiple simultaneous showings. If you make copies for people outside your building, you are distributing the video, and distribution rights are not ordinarily granted. The other school can *lend* you the tape to view, however.

Taping. A lot of misinformation floats around about what may be taped and what may be retained. The number one question to ask when trying to determine a tape's status is "Who taped this and when?" Many court cases have determined that a private individual may tape—for the purposes of "time shifting"—anything broadcast over the public airwaves or from cable channels to which the individual subscribes. The person may then retain the tapes without penalty. But the tape is for the use of only that individual, his or her immediate family, and their circle of friends.

Schools and libraries are not permitted such liberal taping. For school use, programs may be freely taped from regular broadcast channels. Broadcast channels are those VHF and UHF channels one can ordinarily receive via a regular television antenna. If a particular channel is simultaneously rebroadcast on cable, the actual tape may be made from the cable transmission. This can be an advantage in instances when the cable signal is better than the broadcast signal, or when the VCR is already hooked up to the cable instead of an antenna.

But what about all those wonderful cable channels? Disney or A & E or Discovery or Animal Planet? There are no fair use rights for exclusively cable channels. Decisions to tape a particular program must be researched on the basis of granted rights. Since reproduction rights reside with the copyright holder, the ability of a school to tape a program and retain it for any

Q: May a program taped off the air be shown twice in 10 days? For example, if a teacher has four sections of a class, can he show it to only two of them? Must he show it to those four sections as part of the same lesson, or may it be divided?

A: Under the fair use exemption, a program taped off the air may be shown twice in a 10-day period. If the tape cannot he *shown* in a single class period, the showings may certainly be divided. As long as each class sees the entire program no more than twice in the 10-day period, you should be okay. All four sections may see the taping.

amount of time is wholly at the will of the copyright holder. Many of these channels offer educators' guides that enumerate the available rights on a program-by-program basis. *Kidsnet*, Discovery Network's *Educator Guide*, and *Cable in the Classroom* magazines also offer retention rights information and addresses of producers to make it easier for you to request permissions and supplemental materials. See Appendix C for addresses and phone numbers of these reference sources.

Satellite programming will have the same restrictions as cable broadcasts. Programs broadcast by satellite may not be taped for school use without specific permission of the copyright holder. Deliberately de-scrambling encrypted satellite signals is a federal offense.

The location of the taping has no effect on the legality of school use. A teacher or librarian or student may tape programs at school or at home. If a librarian is taping a program, that taping must be at the request of a specific teacher or student. In other words, a librarian cannot tape a program just because she knows someone will ask for it sometime. We all know a teacher who will come into the library the day after a program airs, saying something like, "Gee, it was so good! You wouldn't happen to have that on tape, would you?" If you have taped the program at the specific request of another teacher, you may lend the tape; otherwise, you will have to refuse. Maybe the next time a program airs, the teacher will be better prepared.

Copies taped off-air must include all copyright information, usually included in the credits at the end of the program. The program need not be shown in its entirety, but the program itself must not be edited or altered from its original content. In other words, using the fast forward button on the VCR is acceptable, but editing or shortening the program tape is not always legal, especially if it removes the copyright information.

As you accept taping requests from teachers, keep one requirement in mind: The same teacher may not tape, or request to be taped, the same program multiple times, no matter how many times the program is rebroadcast. A common example would be a teacher's taping a program and showing it to his class. He erases the tape when the 45-day limit expires. The next year the program is rebroadcast and he tapes the program again. This second taping may not be used with students unless the copyright holder gives written permission.

Is this significant? Certainly. An Arizona school district settled a copyright infringement suit alleging that tapes had been made off-air and had not been erased at the end of the 45-day retention period. The Association for Information Media and Equipment (AIME) vigorously pursued the case, eventually receiving significant monetary damages from the district as well as a commitment to follow copyright regulations strictly in the future (AIME, p. 1). AIME is known as an industry watchdog, and given the slightest inkling that a district is in violation of copyright, it will intervene on behalf of its member companies.

So how does one protect oneself and the school from inadvertent infringement in this area? The best suggestion would be to create and maintain a log of taping and use requests (Figures 4.5 and 4.6). This database will contain a history of all off-air tapes used by a particular teacher. While it is possible to manually log tapings, a computer database is the most efficient method of maintaining this type of record. Create fields for teacher, program, channel or network, broadcast date or date taped, and retention rights. When a teacher submits another taping request (or presents a home-taped video), sort the database on the teacher's name and check earlier requests. It will be easy to find a duplication by that teacher. Remember that this database will grow. It isn't a database that can be trashed at the end of each school year. Tapings are cumulative. Once a teacher has taped a particular program (meaning episode or single broadcast), that teacher may not tape the same program again without express permission, even if the program is rebroadcast many months or years later.

Retention. Once a program is taped, when must you use it? The legal restrictions on retention are extremely strict. A taped program may be kept for a maximum of 45 consecutive days. Of that 45 days, students may view the program only during the first10 school days. (Note that student use considers school days, but total time counts consecutive days, including weekends and holidays.) Even those first 10 days are prescribed: once for instruction, once for reinforcement. No other viewings are possible under the fair use guidelines. During the remaining 35 days of the 45-day period, the program may be used only for evaluation of the program by teachers. The program may be retained beyond the 45-day period only if explicit written permission has been received from the copyright holders. Lacking such permission, you must erase or destroy the tape at the end of the 45-day period.

Note that these so-called "fair use" rules apply only to programs taped off regular broadcast channels. Cable or satellite programs that permit limited school use may impose specific retention restrictions that may be more liberal or narrower than the standard 10/45-day fair use, e.g. three days, one year, or life-of-tape. Check program guides and cable-in-education periodicals for specific details on each program.

There are, of course, "special" situations that must be dealt with vis-a-vis copyright. What about a student who was ill and missed an in-class showing? Could another showing be arranged for that student? Probably. Since the library is a place for instruction, and the librarian is certainly an instructor or one directed by the regular instructor, the librarian could arrange a make-up showing of the tape to the student, but only during the first 10 days after the program is taped. The fair use guidelines still apply to the 10-day play limit. If the student does not return until after the 10-day limit has expired, the student will have to rely on other methods to get the information presented in the program.

Home Taping. As long as a program is taped and housed in the library, the librarian can be assured that the tape will be properly logged and will be erased at the end of the 45-day period. But what about home-taped programs brought to school

Figure 4.5

Off-Air Video Log Sample

Teacher	Program	Channel	Date	Rights
Miller	Whale Watch	PBS	9/3/00	fair use
Armand	Using a ruler	NBC	9/5/00	fair use
Raney	The Vietnam experience	Life	9/16/00	7 day
Kyser	National Geographic special	PBS	9/17/00	life/tape
Miller	Oprah	NBC	9/20/00	fair use

Figure 4.6

Off-Air Video Log

Teacher	Program	Channel	Date	Rights

by teachers and students? It makes no difference where the program was taped. What affects school use of taped television programming is the source of the broadcast (broadcast, cable, or satellite) and the date of the taping. The 10/45-day rules apply, no matter who makes the tape or where it is taped. In other words, if a teacher tapes a program in December, but wants to show it in May, such a showing would not be permitted under fair use, and specific, written permission from the copyright holder would be required. Where the program was taped makes no difference at all.

So how does the librarian know the specific details of tapes brought into the building by teachers and students? While it is certainly possible to follow a "don't ask, don't tell" policy in regard to outside video, there would be no documentation should a tape ever be challenged. The best alternative is to require a signed affidavit stating the date and channel on which the program was taped (Figure 4.7).

Copies of Off-Air Recording. In some cases, one program might be appropriate for more than one class at a time; for example, a documentary might be suitable for all the American history classes to view. Not all school buildings are fortunate enough to have a centralized video distribution system that allows a single tape to be shown in multiple classrooms. In such an instance, the school may make copies of the off-air taping, one for each classroom that would need to view the program at the same time. Each copy must have the same off-air taping notices and copyright information attached, and each copy is subject to the same time restrictions as the original. For example, if a tape were made on Sunday, the third day of the month,

---

Figure 4.7

Off-Air Recording Verification

This tape_____
was recorded off-air (circle one) by me/for me on channel_____
on (date)_____. The 10th consecutive school day from the recording date is _____. I may use this recording only once in relevant teaching activities. I may repeat the showing only once for reinforcement. The 45th day after the recording date will be _____. Between the 11th and the 45th days, this tape may be used for teacher evaluation only. It will not be shown to students during this period unless permission has been received from the copyright owner. I made _____ copies of this recording. Each copy is accompanied by this statement. This recording will be erased/destroyed no later than the 45th day indicated above.

Teacher_____

Library Staff_____

Date_____

Signature indicates the statement above has been read and understood.

and the copies of the original recording were made on Tuesday, the fifth, all showings to students from all of the tapes would have to be counted as if all the tapes were made on Sunday the third. The 45-day requirement would also apply to all of the copies, counted from the date of the original recording.

Graphics

The term "graphics" can cover a lot of territory: paintings, photographs, lithographs, serigraphs, etchings, maps, diagrams, charts. Posters and illustrations can all be considered graphics. Graphics pose a major source of potential copyright problems for schools. Section 106 of the copyright law reserves six rights to the copyright owner: reproduction, adaptation, distribution, performance, display, and digital audio transmission. For graphics, the rights of reproduction, adaptation, and display are the most problematic for schools. In certain instances, reproduction of graphic material may fall under the fair use provisions. Making a single copy of a graph or illustration from a book is acceptable if the copy is for personal research or study, and multiple copies of a single graphic are authorized for a class under the following fair use guidelines:

- Copying must be at the instance and inspiration of the teacher and so close in time to the required use that there is not time to request and receive permission;

- The copy is for only one course in the school;

- There are not more than nine occurrences of multiple copying for that course; and

- Not more than one graphic is copied per book or periodical.

Adaptation is a bigger dilemma. Graphics producers make much money from adapting their works for other media. Disney characters adorn everything from drinking cups to nightshirts. Cartoon and advertising graphics decorate paper goods, greeting cards, T-shirts, and billboards. All of these appealing images are attractive to children, and teachers wish to capitalize on their students' recognition of the popular characters and themes. This desire is all the more realistic because virtually every teacher has available the means to incorporate these designs in bulletin boards, handouts, notes to parents, and other decorative uses in the classroom or library. Copyright law doesn't look kindly on such unauthorized uses. By taking an artist's work and enlarging, modifying, or converting it to another medium, a teacher usurps the creator's (or more accurately, the copyright holder's) right to determine how the image will be used.

The library may be a contributory agent in most school-based instances of copyright violation in this area. The primary tool in this misdeed is either the opaque projector or the overhead projector. If the librarian lends that equipment with the knowledge that it will be used to infringe copyright, the librarian is considered a contributory violator because he knows that copyright is going to be infringed and nevertheless contributes to the misdeed. As a contributory offender, the librarian or anyone else with knowledge that the infringement is taking place could be liable for damages. A good plan would be to post the standard copyright warning notice usually affixed to photocopiers and other equipment that could be used to make contraband copies, adaptations, or derivations. The wording of these notices is specified by law, and is reprinted in Appendix D. Preprinted adhesive labels and stand-up signs are sold by the major library supply houses. The librarian who contributes to a copyright violation by lending a projector could make a case that the opaque projector and the overhead projector could be considered "unsupervised reproduction equipment." Libraries (as opposed to schools) aren't held liable for unsupervised reproduction equipment, so the librarian might have a viable defense against contributory liability if the standard disclaimer is attached to any library-owned equipment capable of making reproductions.

Graphic infringements occur when:

■ A teacher uses the opaque projector to enlarge a greeting card illustration for a bulletin board decoration.

■ A librarian photocopies an image from a coloring book as part of a worksheet she is creating.

■ The PTA uses a pantograph or overhead projector to enlarge a poster to wall size as a hall decoration.

■ The art teacher creates stuffed animals of popular picture book characters.

■ The principal scans a cartoon from a magazine into the PTA newsletter.

■ The cheerleading squad creates a paper "run-through" for the basketball team. The "run-through" features a popular cartoon character dressed in the team uniform.

As you can see, the potential for copyright infringement of graphics is great. The best prevention is to insist on original or public domain graphics. The Internet discussion group for school librarians, LM_NET, carried the following message from Corinne Smith, director of audiovisual services at Penn State University. Dealing with copyright of visual material on a daily basis, she has a unique perspective on this issue:

> So far, there have been no comprehensive guidelines issued regarding the scanning or importing of copyrighted materials into your own work—except for the obvious "derivative work" that you are making, presumably illegally.
>
> Most of us live by the rule of asking permission for everything we copy into computer or interactive video programs, even if we're just going to use it in a classroom situation. Some folks have charged us for classroom use, others are just happy we asked for permission.
>
> As for copying fictional character images, you're playing with fire there! Both Disney and Warner Brothers have lawyers combing the country just looking for violations. Their cartoons are both copyrighted and trademarked, so they can get you any way they want to.

Look at Garfield or Snoopy cake pans, even, and you'll see some sort of copyright notice on the box it came in. Look at those nifty Bugs Bunny and Tasmanian Devil cartoon shirts, and you'll see a copyright and trademark notice at the bottom of the shirt. The latest story I heard about fictional characters involved an "illegitimate" Barney imitator who appeared at a local restaurant. The restaurant was issued a cease-and-desist order because that was not a legal Barney running around to greet the kids.

The short version of this message is: for text, get permission to scan it, no matter how much you're using or for what purpose. And don't randomly copy cartoons or images!

Impact of New Technologies

Emerging technologies in schools will ultimately impact our awareness of copyright issues. Until the law is revised, copyright considerations of these untried technologies will necessarily be culled from the law in its current state. Briefly, here are some emerging technologies and a basic explanation of copyright factors to consider in their use:

Closed captioning. There has been much discussion of the legality of adding closed captions to existing video. Some experts argue that adding the special digital coding required for this feature results in a "derivative work" (Sinofsky, Kruppenbacher). Such a derivative work would not be in compliance with copyright. Kruppenbacher, ITV program coordinator at the National Technical Institute for the Deaf, argues that, in order to make a closed-captioned copy, one must make a working copy to which one adds the necessary encoding. He contends that the working copy is, in itself, a violation of copyright.

However, Congressman Robert Kastenmeier stated during congressional arguments on the Copyright Revision Act of 1976 that the legislative intent of the law would specifically allow the making of a working copy with closed captioning in an institution serving the hearing- impaired, as long as the copy stayed within the institution requiring it. The copy must necessarily be restricted from general use, but it might be shared among other institutions serving hearing-impaired populations (Official Fair Use Guidelines, 1987, p.17).

Such diverse opinions put use of this technology in the gray area. If your building has a population of hearing-impaired students, you would probably be safe in closed-captioning your videos that aren't already so encoded. Keep in mind the guidelines Congressman Kastenmeier set forth as parameters and you will probably not be challenged. If still in doubt, consult a copyright attorney.

Scanning. From inexpensive hand-held devices to appliances resembling personal photocopiers, scanners have made it possible to convert both print and graphic material to digital (computer readable) format. Converting from paper to digital format is really an adaptation—one of the six rights of a copyright holder.

In using a scanner, keep in mind the following:

- The material you scan may be protected by copyright. You may not convert print material into digital form without permission of the copyright holder. (Copying in the form of a brief quotation in a scholarly paper is an exception.) Naturally, if you own the copyright of the material you are scanning, you may scan to your heart's content.

- Copying graphic materials such as illustrations or cartoons is also considered a change of format, and as such is not within the law. Modifying an image into something slightly (or even not so slightly) different is also a violation of the law. While one may find it hard to believe, there are certain electronic "fingerprints" that make it possible to determine the origin of an electronic image. While you may believe an image to be modified beyond recognition, it may still be possible to trace its origins.

- There exist collections of public domain clip art, as well as collections for sale. Public domain art may be scanned and used, while purchased clip art may be used in the print version only with permission from the artist or copyright holder. Scanning print clip art would constitute changing format, a right reserved to the copyright holder unless specifically released.

Video Distribution. Video distribution is a type of closed-circuit network in which a classroom teacher (usually) controls video being sent from centralized equipment in the building. Videos are loaded into centrally housed players and are either started at a pre-determined time or are started by the teacher requesting the program. The advantage of the technology is that one doesn't have to roll equipment all over a building, and there is some control over the amount and type of video being used in a building. The primary disadvantage is that since the librarian is usually the person loading and perhaps starting the videos, she becomes a part of the copyright compliance loop.

According to Mary Brandt Jensen, law librarian and law professor, the library or librarian can be considered a contributory agent if "the library caused, assisted, encouraged, or authorized the patron to do the infringing act or was in a position to control the use of the copyrighted work by the patron" (Jensen, p. 150). Obviously, if the library is the site of a video that is being used in violation of copyright law, the library would have to produce considerable evidence that it was unaware of the nature of the video in order to be held blameless.

The author solved the problem of questionable videotapes in the video distribution system by requesting certain documents from teachers before the tapes were played:

- If the tape to be played is owned by the library, all the teacher needs to submit is a copy of the lesson plan showing the link between the lesson and the video. Since the building librarian is familiar with the curriculum of the various grades and classes, it is quite obvious if someone is showing video that is outside of the assigned curriculum, so he could be extra vigilant in these circumstances, perhaps requesting the advice of the administrative staff as to the legality of the showing.

■ If the tape to be shown was rented from a local video store, the teacher still must meet the fair use requirements of the law in order to use the tape in class.

■ If the tape to be played was taped off-air, the teacher must submit a verification of fair use compliance.

Taping off-air, in contrast to taping from cable, is permissible within strict fair-use guidelines. Those guidelines were discussed in the section on off-air taping. Programs taped by the library staff at the request of teachers should be clearly labeled as copyrighted material, and both the record date and erase date explicitly noted on the tape. Presenting a home-taped video to be played in the video distribution system places the librarian's legal life in the hands of another. To assume that all tapes brought to the library are within the legal limits for fair use is naive. If the teacher were to play an illegal tape and be caught, the copyright owner would have a potential case against the librarian as a contributory infringer since the librarian assisted in the illegal display.

Educators can make a modest effort to protect themselves and their schools by requesting disclosure forms from persons wishing to play video through the centralized system. With such verification on file, the school should have a modicum of protection if the tape is later found to be out of compliance. (Figure 4.8) Additionally, a copy of the teacher's lesson plan showing direct correlation of the film to the day's lesson is a good idea.

Digital Video Servers. This emerging technology is so new that everyone employing it is a pioneer–and a potential test case. Few know how the courts will interpret the uses of this technology, but here is a casual assessment. When converting analog (tape) videos into digital (hard disk) storage, one must first convert the format of the video. Format conversion is an adaptation, creating a derivative work. This is a violation of one of the rights of the copyright holder. In addition, the purpose of the conversion is to distribute the video, another right of the copyright holder.

Figure 4.8

Video Release for Middletown High School

I do hereby grant permission to _____

NAME OF TEACHER

to use these videotapes_____

_____

_____

_____

at Middletown High School. It is agreed by myself, as owner of the tapes, and the teacher, as representative of Middletown High School, that the tapes will be shown only for direct instruction, and will not be copied or altered in any way. Neither Middletown High School nor the teacher will charge any fees to any person to view any of the tapes listed above. The teacher named above will be singly responsible for any damage or fees incurred in the use of the above described tapes.

Owner_____

Date_____ Teacher_____

Chapter 5

Multimedia

Multimedia—a copyright infringement nightmare! In creating a multimedia presentation, the user is likely to deal with copyrights on all aspects of the production that aren't actually originated by the author: video, graphics, music or other sound recording, and computer software. Multimedia was invented after the latest revision of copyright law. There are no definitive court cases in this arena, but thanks to the hard work of a group of media producers, publishers, and media consumers, a set of clear-cut guidelines on the use of multimedia in education was approved late in 1996. These guidelines outline the limits of acceptable use of copyrighted materials in fair use situations. The guidelines are not law, just as the fair use guidelines are not law. The guidelines are simply an agreement between those who own the copyrights and those who wish to use the copyrighted materials on what will be permitted under a claim of fair use. Compliance under the guidelines doesn't mean the use is "legal." It means that the copyright holder agrees not to sue someone who uses her materials within these limits.

In order to create a multimedia work, virtually all the relevant material must be transferred to digital format, either disk, laser disk, or CD-ROM. Music, video or still images, and graphics all have different copyrights. And while you may own a CD recording, for example, all you really own is the right to listen to the music until the disk breaks or wears out. You don't own the rights to convert any of that material into another format such as tape or computer disk.

Even some material that might be considered to be in the public domain may have restrictions. Many movie stars made films promoting war bonds, for example. And those films are in the public domain—but only for the purpose of selling war bonds. To use the likeness of any of the stars, you would need to get permission from whoever owns the rights to the likeness (Schneider, p. 33).

The fair use exemption allows some materials to be used in an educational context, but only in the manner in which they were created. For example, you may show a videotape to a class without making special licensing arrangements, providing it meets the face-to-face teaching requirement and the other specified fair use restrictions. But were you to edit that tape so that the scenes were in jumbled order, you would have created a derivative work, and there is no fair use of this application.

The new agreement on Fair Use Guidelines for Educational Multimedia provides concrete limits on the types and amounts of material that may be included in works created by teachers and students. When speaking of fair use and multimedia, one must follow the four tests of fair use that apply to *all* uses of copyrighted materials in schools. Additionally, one of the first notations in the guidelines is that all materials used in derivative works should be properly cited as being taken from the works of others. The guidelines also state that multimedia works made from the copyrighted materials of others may be used only in support of the education of students in nonprofit educational institutions.

Retention and Access

Note: All references to multimedia works are to productions that include copyrighted materials.

Q: Can I take a student's multimedia project to a teacher's workshop outside the school district to use as an example if I obtain the student's and parent's permission?

A: If the student did all the work on the project—there is no copyrighted material included in the project that the student did not create—the permission of the student and parent is all that is required. If, however, the project includes copyrighted material used by the student under the multimedia fair use guidelines, only the student may use the project for workshops. The teacher may not retain copies of the work for any reason.

Obviously, any multimedia production in which the teacher or student creates all the text, data, sounds, and graphics would be totally under the control of the creator. The guidelines permit multimedia works made by students to be used in the class for which they were created, and also retained in portfolios maintained by the student for job interviews, college applications, and other purposes. Teachers may use the multimedia presentations they create in face-to-face instruction, or they may assign students to view the presentations on their own.

If a multimedia work is to be used over a network, several factors come into play. To ensure that only students enrolled in the course may see the program, some type of security is required. Students must log in or provide some other evidence of identity. In addition, the network over which the program is transmitted must have in place a means to prohibit copying of the program. If there is no such safeguard, the program may be used on the network for only 15 days. After that time, the program disk may be checked out to students, but only with a warning that the program may not be copied.

Teachers may display their own multimedia programs at conferences and workshops, and they may retain the programs they create in portfolios for job interviews, evaluations, and other uses. There is a finite limit to an educator's right to keep a work created from copyrighted material, however. While a student may keep a work indefinitely, a teacher may keep a work for only two years from the time of its first use with a class. Beyond the two-year window, permission to retain or use the material is required for *each* portion of copyrighted material used in the presentation. In other words, for teachers, after two years there is no more fair use of the material used in that particular production.

Here are some typical scenarios to illustrate the retention guidelines:

- A teacher creates a multimedia presentation to illustrate a point of his curriculum. The production uses some copyrighted sounds and graphics. The presentation is so successful that the teacher wishes to demonstrate his work at a national conference of teachers. Such a use is within the multimedia fair use guidelines, provided that the display is within two years of the teacher's first use of this production for his classes.

- A student creates a multimedia work utilizing copyrighted materials. The presentation is such an excellent example of student work on this topic that the teacher would like to put the presentation up on the school's network for other students to view for reference, and as an example of how a presentation should be made. This use is permitted only if the audience for this presentation is limited to students enrolled in the class. Some type of network security (passwords, access restrictions) must be in place to restrict access to students in the class.

- A teacher wishes to display an exemplary student multimedia production at an open house, technology fair, or science fair. The production incorporates some copyrighted material. Use of copyrighted materials is permitted for class use only. The guidelines do not allow public performances of materials under fair use.

Quantity Limits

The guidelines specify the amounts of different types of copyrighted materials from a single source that may be used in all multimedia projects created in the course of a term. In other words, from any one video, recording, or database, a specific limit is assigned that a student or teacher may not exceed in a single year or term. Students, especially students in grades K-6, are granted more leeway in their use of copyrighted material. Should a teacher reach this theoretical limit, any additional material in a presentation would require permission.

A concrete example of this rule would be the teacher who uses several images from a library book to create a multimedia presentation for his class. The number of images used reaches the limit assigned in the guidelines for this type of material. Before the term is finished, however, the teacher wishes to use additional materials from the same book for another multimedia presentation to his students. Any use of materials in a single term beyond the limits will require specific permission for each item. The teacher will need to request permission in advance before he may use the additional images.

The limits are:

- Motion media (film, video, television): Up to 10 percent or three minutes, whichever is less, of an individual program.

- Text (prose, poetry, drama): Up to 10 percent or 1000 words, whichever is less, of a novel, story, play, or long poem. Short poems less than 250 words may be used in their entirety. Only three poems by one poet or five poems by different poets from an anthology may be used. For poems longer than 250 words, only three excerpts from one poet or five from works by different poets in an anthology are permitted.

- Music, lyrics, and music video: Up to 10 percent but not more than 30 seconds from a single work (or combined from separate extracts of a work). It makes no difference if the work is being used as a musical work on its own or is an incidental accompaniment to some visual material. If a video clip has music in the background and you can't separate the music from the visual material, you will be restricted by the 30-second limitation for music. If the music is altered in any way, the dominant melody must be maintained and the basic character of the work preserved.

- Illustrations, cartoons and photographs: A work may be used in its entirety but only if no more than five images from a single artist or photographer are used in a multimedia work. In addition, if images are taken from a single collective work, no more than 10 percent or 15 images may be used.

- Numerical data sets (computer databases or spreadsheets): Up to 10 percent or 2,500 fields or cells, whichever is less, may be used from a copyrighted database.

How Many Copies?

An educator may make only two copies (including the original) of the multimedia work. An additional copy may be made if one of the copies is lost, stolen, or damaged. If more than one person creates the multimedia work, each may have one copy of the work. Each copy may be retained as long as is permitted for the type of author (student or teacher). See the section on retention and access for the specific lengths of time.

Other Restrictions

The opening screen of the multimedia work and any accompanying printed materials must contain a notice that the work contains copyrighted materials under the fair use exemption of U.S. Copyright Law. While teachers and students may make alterations to copyrighted material if the purpose is to support specific educational objectives, the author must clearly indicate that such alterations have been made.

The power of multimedia and the computer applications that support it also provide powerful liability for the users. While you have the capability to grab a frame from a film or extract a single face from a photograph or isolate an instrument from the accompaniment of a popular song, you may not exceed the limits imposed in the multimedia guidelines without permission from whoever owns the rights to those items.

Guidelines to remember when creating multimedia presentations:

- Students and teachers may use copyrighted material in multimedia presentations if quantity limits are observed.

- Students and teachers may use copyrighted material in multimedia presentations if they support direct instruction.

- Students and teachers may keep the multimedia presentations they create for class, though teachers face a two-year limit.

- Specific limits are established for the amount of material that may be used in multimedia presentations, based on the original medium.

Best Advice: Invest in clip art, music, and video sold expressly for multimedia productions, or create your own. The multimedia collections are always copyright-cleared for such applications. Clip art books would fall under the "illustrations" portion of the guidelines, since one would have to scan or otherwise digitize the images to include them in a multimedia presentation.

Chapter 6

Satellite and Distance Learning

Neither of these technologies existed when the copyright law was written, so any advice given in these areas comes from extrapolating interpretations of educational use of other technologies. While there are some existing regulations regarding distance learning, the Digital Millennium Copyright Act will ultimately have more impact on distance learning than on any other recent development.

Satellite Transmissions

Keep the following in mind as you deal with satellite transmissions:

- Deliberate unscrambling of an encrypted satellite signal for which subscription fees have not been paid is a serious crime, similar to theft of cable television service. Unencrypted (also called "open") satellite transmissions may also be protected by the Electronic Communications Privacy Act of 1986, known as ECPA. This law protects electronic communications not intended for the general public. There is no fair use for satellite transmissions, live or taped. Materials you license or to which you subscribe will be governed by the agreement you sign. You are entitled to do whatever your license or contract stipulates: tape, retain, rebroadcast.

- Transmission of video or audio via satellite or distance learning equipment goes far beyond the boundaries of the local classroom or school building (as opposed to a video distribution system that stays within the building.) Once a transmission goes beyond the local building, the fair use exemption is lost and public performance rights come into play. Clear all broadcasts of video or audio that extend outside the local campus, even if both ends of the transmission are classrooms. Naturally, if you create the video you transmit, you can do anything you like with it as long as you own all the content.

- Recording from satellite, providing the appropriate access and permission have been granted, will usually be governed by a contractual agreement. For example, a well-known video producer regularly broadcasts its videos by satellite. Subscribers may tape any of the broadcasts for evaluation purposes, but they may retain only an agreed-upon number of the tapes, for which they pay a set fee. The terms of the retention and subsequent copying are part of the contract. Fair use does not enter into this transaction, and intercepting the videos without a contract is considered piracy. There is no fair use for satellite broadcasts. Each use will require specific permission and probably licensing fees. Check the University of Texas System Office of the General Counsel Web site <http://www.utsystem.edu/OGC/IntellectualProperty/distance.htm> for more detailed information regarding copyright changes in this arena.

Distance Learning

While fair use of audiovisual materials is permitted in face-to-face teaching, they are not automatically allowed when the teacher and the students are in different locations. In a face-to-face setting, the instructor can read a poem, play a song, show a film, or many other teaching activities permitted under the face-to-face exemption. Once the students are removed from the presence of the teacher, however, these exemptions fall away. Section 110(2) details the requirements for distance learning (synchronous transmission of teaching activities in real time to distant students in limited locations), and educators are not generally pleased with the limits. When these rules were written, however, the primary form of distance learning was television, in real time. Distance learning has changed considerably since the act was established, and current limitations may not be reasonable for the types of learning activities that occur in an Internet-based distance class, for example.

At the same time the Multimedia Fair Use Guidelines were being negotiated, a similar set of guidelines for distance learning were under discussion as part of the CONFU working group. Unfortunately, the participating parties were not able to agree to even basic fair use limits, and the group disbanded. The need for some form of agreement was apparent to Congress, however, and as part of the Digital Millennium Copyright Act, Congress charged the Registrar of Copyright to hold hearings with all interested parties regarding what would be reasonable and fair in the use of copyright-protected materials in distance education. The registrar's report would be used to propose legislation. The 30-page-plus report was released in the spring of 1999–an encouraging look to the future of distance learning if the bill that will be drafted resembles the report, and if the bill is enacted. In the meantime, those of us who teach at a distance are restricted quite severely unless we obtain permission for each item we use.

Until new rules regarding copyright are enacted, these are "best practices" when using copyright protected materials in distance learning:

- Instructors may show pictures, charts, graphs, text, and other nonmotion media as long as the works are "nondramatic." "Dramatic" literary works such as plays may not be read or performed.

- Instructors may play "nondramatic" musical works, such as concerti, rock music, and instrumental music of many types, but not opera or musicals since they are "dramatic."

- This section of the law specifically excludes audiovisual works, so films, videos, and filmstrips may not be permitted in distance learning situations.

- The above suggestions are based on section 110(2), which deals with distance learning; however one may also apply the four tests of fair use to a proposed use. If the four-test analysis comes out favorably, an educator might prefer to claim a use was fair on the general fair use coverage rather than the specific rules of distance learning.

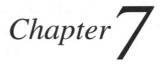

Chapter 7

Computer Software

When the present version of the copyright law was adopted in 1976, computers were huge machines in refrigerated rooms. Few but the most visionary foresaw the emergence of computers as a household or personal appliance—certainly not the Congress as they moved through their deliberations. The 1976 copyright law offered protection to computer programs only as a new form of literary work. By 1980, however, computer programs received expanded protection under Section 117 of the newly revised statute.

Making unauthorized copies of computer software has become a serious issue in recent years. A revision of the law in 1992 brought software piracy to felony status, with fines up to $250,000 for systematic violations. The "No Electronic Theft" (Net) Act, passed in 1997, eliminated a loophole for those who provide contraband copies of software via the Internet and other networks. Those who willfully pirate software $2,500 or more in value are subject to copyright infringement charges, whether or not a profit is made.

License vs. Copyright

While most software (even "shareware") is copyrighted, the purchase of software is usually governed by a license agreement as well as by copyright law. When purchasing a book, the purchaser does not own the book but merely the paper, the ink and binding, and the right to read the words until that copy of the book wears out. The same holds true with software. The purchaser does not own the software, but rather the right to use the software in a manner described in a license agreement, usually included in the documentation of the software package. Reading and understanding the license agreement is an important part of acquiring a new package. Once accepted, these restrictions govern all use of the software.

There are several forms of license agreements: signed agreements, usually on some sort of warranty registration; implied licenses; and so-called "shrink-wrap" licenses. Implied licenses are included in the software packaging, usually as a part of the documentation or as a separate sheet. These licenses usually say something like "Use of the software after reading the license terms implies acceptance." If you don't care for the terms of the license, the manufacturer will usually allow return of the package for a refund. Shrink-wrap licenses are often visible through a plastic wrap on the software package. A similar type of license is called "click wrap" because the license appears when the software is installed. The user must click on an acknowledgement of the license to complete the software installation. The wording of both of these licenses will state that the user is bound by the conditions of the license if he opens the shrink-wrap or clicks the "accept" button. There is a degree of controversy about such default contracts. Some attorneys indicate that if one is given the opportunity to return software once the details of the license are known, the license may be valid. Know your rights in your state.

If the signed license agreement is returned to the software company, or if you click on the button that signals acceptance, you will be legally bound by the restrictions imposed therein. This license agreement may supersede some standard rights under copyright. It may also grant some extra privileges, such as the ability for the person on whose computer the software is installed to install it on a laptop or home computer as well. This permission is by no means a right, but a gracious offer on the part of the software company. Read the fine print to determine if, and what, permissions you may have.

Some license agreements grant the purchaser the right to duplicate a specified number of copies—commonly called a limited site license. The software producer allows a discount on the software price, and in return the purchaser uses his own diskettes and labor to make copies. Site licenses are generally specified on purchase orders, hence are legal and binding contracts between the purchaser and the producer. Because the deal involves a contract, producers may be able to work out the exact type of license you desire, even if those particular terms may not be listed on the producer's price sheet. If the producer suspects the purchaser has violated the license agreement, the legal action is more likely to be based on contract law than on copyright, but damages could still be significant if the purchaser is found guilty.

Legitimate Copying vs. Piracy

Illegal copying of computer software is called "piracy." For teachers and students who have computers at home that are compatible with the equipment at school, the temptation is strong to bring home a copy of the school's software so that work can be transferred back and forth. The rules on making copies of computer programs allow only two instances in which copies may be made of programs outside the scope of a valid license agreement.

Q: *I remember hearing from some source several years ago that it was okay to purchase a videotape, make a copy, and circulate the copy while keeping the original in an archive. Is this true?*

A: Since 1976 it has been legal to make backup copies of computer diskettes. There is not now and never has been permission to make backup copies of videos, audiocassettes, phonograph records, or laser discs.

A copy or adaptation may be made if such a copy is an essential part of the operation of the computer program. For example, if the program must be copied to the hard disk of the computer, that copying is acceptable. Since most, if not all, computer programs require the program to copy itself into the computer's memory in order to run, such an "ephemeral" copy is also permitted under this portion of the law. The program erases itself when the program closes. In addition, modifications such as installing a printer driver or other customizations allowed by the software itself are also within the acceptable limits of adaptation.

A copy or adaptation for archival purposes may be made if it is not to be used. This copy can be on disk, diskette, backup CD, or tape. The archival or backup copy should be destroyed if the program is sold or transferred. You may use the backup copy of the software and put the original away for safekeeping, or vice versa. Either is acceptable as long as both copies are not used at the same time. This provision is only for "owners" of software, however, not for licensees, so determine which you are before you make your backups.

Don't forget that the Digital Millennium Copyright Act requires you not to remove copyright management information from protected works, including computer software. A license agreement may contain the copyright management information for a specific software package, so be wary about discarding all that fine print.

Infringement actions similar to those that can occur in the realm of print can also occur with computer software. The Software and Information Industry Association defines several types of software copying to which it objects for which it is willing to prosecute. Here are SIIA's definitions of the types of activities of which to be wary:

Direct Infringement

Anyone who violates any of the exclusive rights of the copyright owner [reproduction, adaptation, distribution to the public, public performance, public display, rental for commercial advantage or importation] violates the copyright or the right of the author (Section 501(a)).
- Downloading software,
- Uploading software,
- Making software available for download, and
- Transmitting software files.

Indirect Infringement

Contributory Infringement. Anyone who knows or should have known that he or she is assisting, inducing or materially contributing to infringement of any of the exclusive rights by another person is liable for contributory infringement.

- Posting of serial numbers,
- Posting of cracker utilities,
- Linking to FTP [file transfer protocol] sites where software may be unlawfully obtained,
- Informing others of FTP sites were software may be unlawfully obtained,
- Aiding others in locating or using unauthorized software,
- Supporting sites upon which the above information may be obtained, and
- Allowing sites where the above information may be obtained to exist on a server.

Vicarious Liability for Infringement by Another Person.

Anyone who has the authority and ability to control another person who infringes any of the exclusive rights and who derives a financial benefit therefrom, is vicariously liable for the infringement of another person.

- ISPs [Internet service providers] who have warez [proprietary software with copy protection removed illegally] or pirate sites on their system.
- ISPs who have pirates for customers.
- System Administrators for newsgroups or IRC [Internet Relay Chat] where pirate activity takes place.

(Software and Information Industry Association,
<www.siia.net/piracy/copyright/risk.asp>)

Computer Documentation

While printed documentation isn't actually part of the electronic program, it is also protected under software copyright. Archival copies are permitted, but multiple copies for classroom distribution, for example, are not permissible without specific permission (TEA, 1984, p.11). Classes such as drafting, word processing, and business applications that use high-power commercial software are likely to be tempted to make copies of command cards, keystroke shortcut sheets, and other handy reference lists included with the printed documentation. Such copying is prohibited unless it is specifically permitted in the license. When negotiating licenses, ask for extra command sheets or request permission to reprint portions of the documentation as necessary.

Single-User Programs

A common act of software piracy in schools is that of purchasing a single-user copy of a program and then installing it on multiple machines. The program may be a grade book, a database manager, a word processor, or an integrated software package. The program may even be as basic as the disk operating system (DOS or System 7) itself. Teachers and administrators rationalize the decision by saying that they aren't making any profit on the deal, and the school certainly can't afford all those single copies. Unfortunately, the end doesn't justify the means. And making more than 10 copies of a program immediately

Q: *I never know what computer will be available when a student asks to use a particular CD-ROM program. Can I install the program on all my computers so it will work on whatever computer is free? The program will not work without the CD in the drive.*

A: This isn't a recommended practice. If your license indicates you may install the software on only one machine, that is specific. If you were to be audited, the audit program would tally each installation of the program. You would have to produce a license for each installation.

Q: *Since single-user CD-ROM programs may not be partially installed on more than one computer even though the CD must be in the computer for actual usage, could the CD-ROM programs be used in this manner if we received permission from the producer or publisher?*

A: The conditions I describe are those allowed under fair use *with no permission.* If you get permission or a license that gives greater rights, you are limited to what the license will (or will not) allow.

raises the penalty for infringement to up to $250,000 in fines and up to five years in prison on felony charges (Marshall, p. 441).

If such multiple loads currently reside on programs in a district, often software producers will sell school districts licenses only, for software at a greatly reduced price. The license includes no disks or documentation, but it legitimizes copies currently residing on the computers.

Some CD-ROMs require that a portion of the program be installed to the local hard disk in order to speed access to the CD. With such an installation, at the time of use one has only to slip the CD-ROM into the drive and the program will work. Unfortunately, loading even a portion of the program on multiple computers without specific exemption is technically a violation of the single-use license.

Multiple Loading vs. Multiple Copies

Some computer programs are contained on one diskette. If the entire program can fit into the active memory (RAM) of the computer, the diskette may be removed from the disk drive during the operation of the program with no ill effects on program operation. Since the diskette is now available, it is technically possible to repeat the process in a second (and third, and . . .) computer. This process is called "multiple loading." It differs from multiple copies of a computer program because the copy exists only in the electronic memory of the computer and is not put onto a diskette or other storage device.

Unless expressly permitted by license, multiple loading is likely a violation of copyright (Official Fair-Use Guidelines, 1987, p. 15). The law does not use this precise term, but the intent of the restrictions on making copies can easily be extended to copying the program into multiple machines.

Some software licenses specifically mention multiple loading as either an acceptable or prohibited practice. In the absence of any mention of multiple loading, though, one must assume that the practice is not permitted under the terms of the contract. Loading a program intended for a single machine onto many also violates the fair use limitation of Section 107, which identifies the loss of potential sales as a justifiable reason for denying unrestricted copies. The copyright holder would be deprived of potential sales of the product if the program is used in multiple machines that otherwise would have used legitimately purchased copies of the software.

To answer the need for multiple copies of educational software, software producers have developed discount pricing agreements for educational institutions, lab packs of multiple copies of the software with a single copy of the documentation, and site licenses allowing restricted duplication of the software by the license holder.

Networking

If the hardware will support it, network options allow multiple computers to share one copy of the software. However, networking software is not covered under fair use. All network and site licenses are contracts negotiated with the sellers—not a right under fair use. The fact that a particular piece of software can operate in a networked environment is immaterial. Networking a piece of computer software always requires a license. And get it in writing!

Some software, particularly CD-ROMs, will permit unlimited networking within a single building. "Building" can be defined as organizational campus—a group of students who have a single administrative head. Many schools, especially high schools, comprise multiple buildings. There may be a central building, a field house, an annex or portable buildings, or a separate gymnasium or auditorium. As long as those buildings compose the physical plant of that organizational unit, any computer in those buildings could qualify to access the CD-ROM under the network site license.

Some school-owned plots of land house two schools, however. An elementary school and a high school might be on the same parcel. They might even share network components. But for license purposes, those are probably two separate schools. If the two schools have separate names and separate administrators, the software people would be able to make an excellent case for their being two entities. In such cases, it is best to be up-front with the software producer when purchasing a license.

Another networking issue that should be considered is how to network CD-ROMs. Many networks employ CD-ROM towers—units attached to the network as independent units to provide data from CD-ROMs to any workstation that requests it. These towers require additional, specialized hardware and software—both relatively expensive and not particularly fast in data delivery. As an option, some network specialists have elected to copy the data from the CD-ROM onto a single large hard disk drive on the network server. Hard disks are much less expensive than CD-ROM towers, and they have the advantage of not requiring special CD-ROM networking software to access them. They also deliver data to the workstation much faster than a CD-ROM drive.

Copyright enters the picture here when you copy the data. You are making an additional copy of the computer program or data. Unless you are specifically permitted in the license agreement to make such a copy (either as a stock part of the license or as a negotiated add-on), making such a copy is contrary to the letter of copyright law.

Software for Free?

Two forms of software may be freely copied without any licenses or agreements. The first type is known as "public domain" software—a computer program that has been released by the author to be freely copied by whoever would like to use it. Such software is often found on Internet FTP sites, computer bulletin boards, and diskettes from computer users' groups and clubs. The title screen of the program or the documentation will indicate the public domain status of the program.

The other form of software that may be freely copied isn't exactly free. Known as "shareware," this software is copyrighted. The author or copyright holder has elected to distribute the software through a try-it-before-you-buy-it method. Shareware software is available through the same channels as public domain software; but once the software has been used and evaluated, the user is expected to register the software and pay a fee for the program—anything from a voluntary donation (sometimes to a charitable organization) up to $100 or so. Some authors give a time frame for this trial period. The software may or may not continue to work at the end of the stated period. Others just say, "If you like it, send money." It's the honor system at its most fragile. If users of shareware fail to register and pay for the software that they retain and use, this method of software distribution may disappear.

Lending Software

In 1990, Congress responded to the complaints of computer software producers that lending and renting of computer software were eroding the market for their products. The Copyright Software Rental Amendments Act was the result. In essence, the act granted to copyright owners (of computer software only) the right to control rental, lease, or lending of their software. However, the law did provide an exemption for nonprofit libraries provided that a warning of copyright is affixed to each package. The Federal Register specified the exact wording of the notice:

Notice: Warning of copyright restrictions

The copyright law of the United States (Title 17, United States Code) governs the reproduction, distribution, adaptation, public performance, and public display of copyrighted material. Under certain conditions specified in law, nonprofit libraries are authorized to lend, lease, or rent copies of computer programs to patrons on a nonprofit basis and for nonprofit purposes. Any person who makes an unauthorized copy or adaptation of the computer program, or redistributes the loan copy, or publicly performs or displays the computer program, except as permitted by Title 17 of the United States Code, may be liable for copyright infringement. This institution reserves the right to refuse to fulfill a loan request if, in its judgment, fulfillment of the request would lead to violation of the copyright law.

The register further states that this notice must be "durably attached" to the package that is loaned to patrons. Some library supply houses sell stickers carrying this required statement. As a final note, remember that this exemption for lending software is for libraries only. Academic departments, administrators, or computer or technology directors do not qualify for this exemption.

The Software Police

While the dreaded software police don't actually exist, the FBI can, and does, investigate and enforce suspected copyright violations as part of its general responsibilities. Since computer software piracy is now punishable as a felony (Marshall, p. 441), prosecution is much more zealous. Representatives of a software publishing firm did, in fact, visit one of the schools in a district where I worked. They asked courteously but firmly to see verification that legitimate copies of their software had been purchased. When the original packages and documentation were produced for their inspection, they thanked the librarian politely and left. They declined to say why they had selected this building for an inspection.

Schools and districts are advised by organizations such as the Business Software Alliance (BSA) and the Software and Information Industry Association (SIIA) to conduct software audits. Essentially this puts someone in the building and district in the position of software policeman. SIIA even offers a school policy recommendation that outlines steps for maintaining records of legitimate copies of software, a software program that logs many of the frequently pirated applications programs into a printed record, and a free kit on how to conduct a self-audit of software.

Such an audit makes employees who put personal software on institutional machines subject to further investigation to determine if such use is within the applicable software licenses. With few exceptions, people may not load copies of software installed at home on school machines as well (under the same license). Vigorous application of a copyright compliance policy could subject employees to disciplinary procedures if they are found in violation of the copyright laws during such an audit.

Two school districts in Texas do surprise software audits of one another. Armed with the SIIA's program, WRQ Express Inventory, SPA Edition, officials from one district appear at a selected school of the other district, acting in the manner of federal marshals. They run the audit program on all computers with hard disks. The program produces a printout of all the executable programs on the drive. The owner of the drive is then requested to produce authentication that each program is legitimate. An official of one of the districts recounted that one individual had many questionable programs on the computer's hard drive. When this employee had not accounted for programs on the computer a month later, an official letter of reprimand went into the person's file. This reciprocal checking is helping to keep both districts in compliance and out of court.

The Impact of New Technologies

Expanding computer-based technology has made application of existing copyright law difficult. The law was written long before CD-ROM, multimedia, and their cousins were invented; hence, many of the recommendations applied to those media are interpolated and extrapolated from existing decisions made concerning other, related media. Bounty hunters notwithstanding, software producers have taken heroic measures to safeguard their significant investment.

Some software producers attempt to enforce their own contract terms by selling software that can count the number of users in a network environment. For example, if the school has paid for a four-user license, the software will allow only that number of concurrent users and no more. Other makers disable or limit features of the software, such as being able to copy information to floppy disk, so that wholesale portions of the copyrighted database cannot be incorporated into someone else's work. These features or limitations should be spelled out in the license agreement and software documentation before the purchase is concluded, so that both the producer and the purchaser understand the requirements and limits of the program and its data.

The recent Digital Millennium Copyright Act has put some teeth into the law about circumventing technical protections. In other words, if software has a password or copy protection scheme, it is now a violation to bypass these protections. There are some complicated exceptions for libraries, but mostly these exceptions are in place so that librarians can inspect items prior to purchasing them. In most instances, evaluation copies are available to let them make sound purchase decisions.

Negotiated CD-ROM licenses are just as binding as computer software licenses. Some may allow for unlimited use within one site, others within a district. Each is valid, and each should be tracked and audited for compliance. External access (by telephone line and modem, for example) is frequently restricted by CD-ROM database producers to students or faculty of the purchasing institution. Keep this in mind when planning school-community partnerships or other networking arrangements. The CD-ROM databases that are so attractive may not be legally shared if the license states "no remote access." This contract supersedes the Section 108 rights of libraries to provide information to anyone who requests it. In essence, by accepting the software license, the purchaser waives other rights under copyright, just as with regular computer software.

Copyright Infringement vs. Plagiarism

Q: I want to use material that I have captured from the Internet and from a CD-ROM. As long as I cite the source, I can copy anything I like, right?

A: Not necessarily. Just citing a source doesn't absolve you of the responsibility to get permission from the copyright owner if you don't qualify for fair use.

A question arises concerning students who download or capture information from CD-ROM or other electronic sources. As in most student situations, students may use all sorts of information for personal research, as long as they cite their sources. The fact that a student has used electronic means to put the information into the product rather than typing or handwriting is irrelevant. The problem here is not copyright infringement, but plagiarism. The student may be operating within fair use to use the copyright protected materials; he is, however, breaking the school's (and society's) code against copying without credit.

(For someone attempting to prove plagiarism, having information in electronic format is actually a blessing. In pre-electronic days, the teacher had to scan printed works hoping to stumble upon the exact suspected text. Now the teacher need only do a simple text search of the source to find all instances of the wording in question.)

Any instance of plagiarism is probably a copyright violation, too, because in the absence of attribution, the student isn't likely to be covered by the fair use exemption. In dealing with ethical issues such as copyright law compliance and plagiarism, it is important for teachers and librarians to emphasize high expectations. Adherence to copyright law and rules against plagiarism should be fully detailed in student codes of conduct, with specific penalties for violations.

Scanners

The scanner is a new computer-based technology that has jolted the world of print copyright. Virtually any image can now be transformed into bits and bytes for incorporation into graphics packages, desktop publishing documents, and multimedia presentations. As stated previously, the original copyright holder retains the rights of reproduction, adaptation, and display, among others. Scanning a copyrighted illustration may be a copyright violation of any of those three rights. A student may use a scanned copyrighted image in a report, but the student must retain ownership of the report once it is graded. The teacher may not retain that report (or a copy of it), nor may he reproduce it for a workshop.

If the work is a multimedia presentation, it may be displayed only for the students and teachers in the class for which it was prepared. Presentation before what would amount to an open audience is considered a public performance. The student may not grant permission for such a performance because, while he owns the copyright to his own portion of the work, he may not give permission for that which he does not own—the copyrighted material he has "borrowed" to enhance his own work.

A staff member cannot scan a cartoon or article into a newsletter for distribution to the faculty or parents. A scanned copy of a famous photograph cannot legally be modified by computer graphics into a similar, or even quite different, image. There is no amount of modification that can be made to an original image to make the format conversion "okay." In short, just because the technology exists to reproduce an item electronically, the user of the technology does not have the right to do so.

Other Infringements

School personnel who lend computer software to persons they know intend to copy it, and school personnel who knowingly lend the necessary equipment to copy software may also be charged with copyright infringement. This situation is known as contributory infringement. Prosecution under this aspect of the law is uncommon, but not unknown. An example of such an act would be a video store selling tapes it knew to be in violation of copyright. They did not make the infringing copies, but they profited by the sale of copies they knew to be illegally made (Berman). A school whose educators use videos they know to be improperly made would be at risk of some sort of enforcement action.

Similarly, a principal who had been notified that an employee was violating copyright but who took no action could be charged with vicarious infringement if the employee knew the actions violated the law. Naturally, any of these cases would have a vigorous defense on several grounds, but the fact remains that one does not actually have to make the copy to be held liable. One must decide for oneself if the risk of suit is worth the activity. Here are some common computer software copyright situations and their legal implications:

■ A teacher comes to the library to ask to install her personal copy of a word processing program on one of the school computers. She will be using the program at home in the evenings and at school during the day, so only one copy will be in use at a time.

In the absence of a license provision permitting such uses, having the same software loaded on two computers even if they are not in use at the same time is not permitted.

■ The technology coordinator wants to save some money on the new building-wide network. In order to avoid the expense of a CD-ROM tower, he proposes to copy the library's CD-ROM discs onto a large hard disk for access.

Copying CD-ROMs onto hard disks for active use is not permitted under the standard software copyright provisions. Many software companies will, however, grant permission to access CD-ROM data in this fashion if asked.

■ A student accesses the Internet from the library and downloads a shareware game from a Web site. He proceeds to give copies of the game to all his friends.

Shareware is a type of copyrighted software, which may be freely distributed. The user of the software must pay a fee if he or she decides to keep the software after trying it. Anyone may give copies of shareware software to others. The ultimate user is the person who is obligated to pay the license fee.

Recommendations

■ Maintain copyright and license records on all programs in the building. If a site license or network copy was ordered, retain a copy of the purchase order as proof of the contract.

■ Make one archival copy of each program and store it off-site. Do not use or circulate the archival copy. One archival copy of software documentation is allowed. More than one requires permission.

■ Don't install non-network software on a network. Installation of software on a network requires a network license.

■ Don't lend equipment that would facilitate copying software. Don't own programs whose sole purpose is to "crack" software protection schemes.

- Refuse to lend software to library patrons who indicate they plan to make infringing copies. At minimum, inform them that the software is protected by copyright and their use of the software is governed by the notice affixed to the package.

- Place appropriate copyright warning stickers on all software circulated from the library.

- Register shareware.

- Enforce multi-user limitations. Install software metering programs or use network operating system security options to monitor licenses.

- Restrict outside access to CD-ROM databases if the license requires only in-house use.

- Monitor use of computer scanners and digitizers. Encourage use of public domain and royalty-free graphics.

Where To Get More Information

The Software and Information Industry Association offers an anti-piracy hotline at 1-800-388-7478. Find them online at <www.siia.net/piracy/report/default.asp>.

The Business Software Alliance also has an anti-piracy hotline at 1-800-688-2721. Their Web address is <www.bsa.org>.

Chapter 8

Interlibrary Loan, Photocopying, Facsimile, and Reserves

This chapter profiles specific requirements that libraries are expected to meet based on the library exemptions detailed in Section 108 of U.S. Copyright Law. School libraries have the best of all possible worlds when it comes to copyright exemptions, because they are permitted both the school and the library exemptions. The downside of this bonus is that libraries must keep track of twice as many sets of regulations. Section 108 provides an assortment of special exceptions for libraries including copying for interlibrary loan, copying at the request of patrons for their personal use, and copying for preservation.

Aside from the regulations discussed below, to qualify for the library exemptions, the library must be open to the public (or to researchers in a field). Most school libraries would meet this requirement based on the definition of "public" discussed earlier. A second requirement of the library exemptions is that all copies made must be made "without any purpose of direct or indirect commercial advantage." All copies made must contain a notice of copyright, and copying must be of single copies on "isolated and unrelated" occasions. A key phrase in the law states that "systematic reproduction or distribution of single or multiple copies" is always prohibited.

Library Copying

If a librarian makes copies of magazine articles or other parts of larger works for patrons to use in personal research, he must observe several points of the law. The copies must become the property of the user. The librarian may not make a copy for a user, then retain the copy once the user is finished. If he makes a copy that he knows will be used for other than personal research, he is at fault.

- The library must display the "warning of copyright" at the point where requests for copies are made. If the patron requests a complete work, the library may make the copies if

- The librarian can determine that a copy for purchase is not available at a fair price;

- The user will keep the complete copy to be made;

- The librarian has no information that the copy will be used for anything beyond personal research; and

- The library displays the "warning of copyright" where copying orders are placed.

Since the passage of the Digital Millennium Copyright Act, libraries that make copies (as opposed to libraries that provide unsupervised copiers) must include with each copy the original notice of copyright included on the item being copied. For a book, that would be the copyright information found on the verso of the title page. Other types of materials will also have copyright information found on the original items that must be included when the librarian makes the copies. She can simply include a photocopy of the information or manually transcribe that information onto the photocopies. If an item being copied has no copyright notice, the librarian must include a statement that the work may be protected by copyright—essentially the statement currently used on the ALA-worded stamp available at library supply houses: *Notice: This material may be protected by Copyright Law (Title 17 U.S. Code)*. In addition, the works copied cannot be pictures or graphics unless those illustrations or diagrams appear in other works, too.

Put a dozen librarians in a room and you will come up with two dozen plans to economize while providing exemplary library service. (All good librarians have a backup plan!) Providing outstanding service can be problematic if the library doesn't have all, or enough, of the items the patrons seek. Many creative ideas have been proposed to provide extra copies of materials, secure materials that libraries don't own, and get materials quickly to patrons who need information immediately. But as with all innovative solutions, new outcomes will be measured against traditional laws. Lawmakers are notoriously slow to adapt current law to new technologies, and until they do so, one must use the old laws and attempt to extrapolate today's legal requirements.

Photocopiers

Librarians are in the business of sharing as much information with as many people as they can. They have made photocopiers available for patrons so they may make copies of whatever information they desire. Copyright law even says that a person may make a single copy of certain information for his own research and education. But what if the photocopier is located in the library, and the patron exceeds the limits of the law? Does that make the library responsible for any infringements committed there?

The answer lies in the location of the copier. The law specifies that libraries are not held accountable for copyright infringements on "unsupervised" copiers. What is "supervised?" "Supervised" isn't defined, but there are some common sense guidelines one can follow:

■ If library staff make the copies, certainly that would mean they are supervising the making of copies, and the library would be liable for any infringements made there.

■ A copier beside the circulation or reference desk could also be considered "supervised" in some instances.

■ A self-service copier across the room from the staff, however, would be independent, even if the library staff maintain the paper and toner in the machine.

Library staff are not held liable for copies made on "unsupervised" copiers if there is an appropriate notice on the copier informing the patron that some materials may be protected by U.S. copyright law. This notice is most often placed on the lid of the copier, where the patron is sure to see it as he places the original on the machine for copying. Many library supply houses have signs or adhesive notices just for the purpose of informing patrons of their responsibilities under the law. The statute does not specify wording in this instance, but the American Library Association suggests the following:

> Notice: The copyright law of the United States (Title 17 U.S. Code) governs the making of photocopies or other reproductions of copyrighted material. The person using this equipment is liable for any infringement.

This notice should be affixed to all equipment capable of making infringing copies: photocopiers, overhead projectors, opaque projectors, computers, videocassette recorders, scanners, audio cassette recorders, fax machines, and any other equipment that can be used to copy video, sound, or print. Placing such a notice in a prominent position on copy-producing equipment can reduce (though never eliminate) the library's and the librarians' exposure to copyright suit if the library's equipment is used by patrons to make infringing copies.

Keep in mind that this exemption applies only to libraries. School-owned copiers in the office, workroom, or department do not have this exemption, so school staff must be especially vigilant about unauthorized copies on all machines.

If the library copier is unsupervised, i.e., users make their own copies on a coin- or card- or even honor-system-operated machine without intervention or supervision by the library staff, a library is not liable for copyright violations. If the school staff makes the copies, or the user consults the library staff on making the copies, the copier is considered to be supervised, and the school will likely be held accountable for the illegal copies. The term "supervised" would also include any copies made by library staff for patrons or school staff, regardless of the location of the copier.

Copies made by library staff must include the original statement of copyright as printed on the item being reproduced. This may be manually transcribed, or it may be a photocopy of the copyright statement on the item. If the item being copied has no statement of copyright, one cannot easily determine if the item is or is not protected by copyright. In such an instance, the copies should be stamped with a notice indicating that the material copied may be covered by copyright, and that appropriate use of copyrighted material is the responsibility of the patron. While no particular wording is specified by law, many libraries use

Notice: This material may be protected by copyright law (Title 17 U.S. Code)

stamped on copies in a conspicuous color. It is especially important to be diligent about including the copyright statement on school- or library-made copies if one wishes to protect the building and its personnel against infringement actions.

Preservation

The Digital Millennium Copyright Act added some positive permissions for libraries dealing with deteriorating, damaged, or obsolete materials. If a work has been damaged or defaced, and an "unused replacement" cannot be purchased at a reasonable cost, the library may make the copies necessary to repair or replace the item. Laura Gasaway, in a presentation to the Texas Library Association in April 2000, explained that if you own a set of encyclopedias, and someone steals or destroys a single volume, and if the publisher will not sell you a single replacement volume, it is reasonable to assume that an unused replacement is not available at a reasonable price. In such an instance, she recommends making the copies necessary to repair or replace the item.

When copying unpublished materials (diaries, family photographs, historical documents, and the like) the copying must be

- For preservation, security, or deposit at a different library (good insurance against fire or other disaster); and

- Be of an original owned by the copying library.

- The subsection on preservation (c) permits copies of any material if:

    - That material cannot be replaced at a reasonable cost, or

    - If the format in which the material is stored is obsolete.

The law considers material to be obsolete "[I]f the machine or device necessary to render perceptible a work stored in that format is no longer manufactured or is no longer reasonably available in the commercial marketplace." Preservation copies can even be digital copies if the copies are not made available to the public outside the library holding the original item. This section would permit a library, for example, to copy Beta-format videotapes into VHS format because the necessary equipment is no longer available on the general market.

Interlibrary Loan

Common sense tells us that by pooling resources, several libraries can share expensive or seldom-used materials. Interlibrary loan has served that function for many years.

As library budgets get tighter, librarians look for creative ways to make the budget dollars stretch a little further. One oft-suggested idea is to spread periodical subscriptions around, each cooperating library taking a portion of the little-used, but still important, titles. When a patron needs something from one of the titles subscribed to by one of the sharing partners, a simple interlibrary loan request will rush the information to the patron. With a fax machine, access to remote documents is almost instantaneous. Sound too good to be true? It is.

At this point in our plan we run afoul of the copyright law. One of the principal tenets of the law is that copying should not affect the market for or value of the copyrighted work. Does securing a needed article or book from a remote site deprive the copyright holder of a sale? Would the patron or the library have bought the title just to have access to that particular article? Does rapid document delivery affect sales of periodical titles? Good questions, and ones that the congressional committee considered when they discussed fair use in the areas of photocopying and resource sharing.

Items available for interlibrary loan would include books, periodicals, and any other work that the library chooses to release from its premises. Copying for interlibrary loan, however, picks up an extensive list of restrictions. Thanks to the Digital Millennium Copyright Act, libraries may not copy a musical work; a picture, sculpture or graphic (unless those items are included as illustrations in a textual item); or a movie or audiovisual work. Text may be copied for interlibrary loan (subject to the CONTU guidelines, below) as may sound recordings. Audiovisual works dealing with news may also be copied for interlibrary loan.

The copying requirements for interlibrary loan are essentially the same as the library copying requirements listed above. Because the 1976 law allowed libraries to participate in interlibrary loan (ILL) arrangements as long as "aggregate quantities" of articles or items received did not substitute for a periodical subscription or other purchase, a group known as the National Commission on New Technological Uses of Copyrighted Works (CONTU) developed a set of guidelines that were adopted as fair and reasonable. Known universally as the CONTU Guidelines, these rules establish operational procedures that should be followed in interlibrary loan copying to assure compliance with the copyright law. The rules are not intended to apply to every situation, but Congress itself declared that they would "provide guidance in the most commonly encountered interlibrary photocopying situations" (Copyright Office, Circular R21, p. 22).

Keep in mind that the CONTU guidelines govern interlibrary loan of periodicals and other works. Intralibrary loan is an entirely different animal. The difference? Primarily funding. The guidelines point to "common funding" as the key element in determining if libraries are part of the same system (Ensign, p. 126). For example, all the schools in a school district would be considered part of a common system and therefore loans among them would be intralibrary loans. Loans between school districts would be interlibrary loans.

In dealing with intralibrary loan, sending a photocopy of an article is handled exactly the same as if the copy were being made in the patron's library by library personnel. Section 108 of the copyright law allows not-for-profit libraries to make single copies of material for patrons as long as there is no commercial advantage, the library is open to the public, and each reproduction includes a notice of copyright.

Caveat: The law, however, has a very specific prohibition against "systematic" copying. The guidelines give the following example of systematic copying: "Several branches of a library system agree that one branch will subscribe to particular journals in lieu of each branch purchasing its own subscriptions, and the one subscribing branch will reproduce copies of articles from the publication for users of other branches." This budget-stretching plan to share periodical subscriptions or reference books among campuses within or outside a school district (or perhaps between the schools and the public library) is not in compliance with the copyright law in any case.

Following the CONTU Guidelines gives a librarian a set of conservative, baseline rules on acceptable copying for inter- or intralibrary loan. These guidelines are mandatory for interlibrary loans. Since maintaining two sets of ILL rules would boggle even the clearest mind, applying those rules to intralibrary loan gives a safe level of ILL practice and consistent operation. The guidelines are very specific and, once implemented, relatively easy to follow. They apply to interlibrary loan copying, not interlibrary loans in which the original material is mailed or delivered to the requesting library. The CONTU Guidelines state that:

The borrowing library must display a "warning of copyright" at the place interlibrary loan orders are accepted. The size and wording of this notice are specified by law. These notices are sold by library supply houses. See Appendix D for exact requirements.

- Only one copy of the requested material may be sent, and that copy must become the property of the requesting patron. Fax delivery thus runs counter to the guidelines, as does retaining a copy for the borrowing library's vertical file.

- The **borrowing** library must abide by the "Rule of Five" (explained in the next section).

- The **borrowing** library must keep records of CONTU-governed loan requests for four years (e.g., on Jan. 1, 2004, the records for 2000 may be discarded). A database, loose-leaf notebook, or card-based record-keeping system can track requests. See examples of forms later in this chapter.

- The **borrowing** library must verify copyright compliance on the ILL request. Most stock ILL forms have a section for copyright compliance, indicating CCL ("Complies with Copyright Law," that is, fair use) or CCG (Complies with CONTU Guidelines, that is, the Rule of Five).

- The **lending** library must mark on each copy that the "request was made in conformity with these guidelines." In general, that means the copy should be stamped with the standard *Notice: This material may be protected by Copyright Law (Title 17 U.S. Code). Complete copyright information must also be included, if available, per DMCA.*

Rule of Five

Q: How many articles from each issue of a periodical is a library allowed to copy for interlibrary loan?

A: The providing library may make any copies requested by other organizations since it is the *requesting* library's responsibility to maintain copyright compliance according to the CONTU guidelines.

Q: For interlibrary loan, can a library request five articles from each issue of a given periodical?

A: The Rule of Five states that during the *current* calendar year you may request up to five copies of articles from the last four calendar years of a periodical *title*. It makes no difference from whom you request the articles.

Periodicals. The CONTU Guidelines pertain to periodical *titles* (as opposed to individual issues) published within five years from the date of the request. Copying older materials may be considered to be fair use on the part of the requesting library. The borrowing library may receive five photocopied articles per periodical title (not per issue) per calendar year. On the standard ILL form, these first five copies may be marked as CCG since they are permitted under the CONTU Guidelines. To give a specific example, in a single year a library that does not subscribe to *Library Talk* could, within these guidelines, request five single articles published within the past five years. Some exemptions apply to the limit of five:

A title "on order." If you have entered an order for a periodical title, you may request unlimited copies from the title under CONTU. The Rule of Five does not apply.

A title at the bindery. If you own the title and you have sent the issues to the bindery, you may request unlimited copies from those issues under CONTU.

Missing issues in an owned volume. If you already own a volume of a periodical and need to request an interlibrary photocopy to supplement a missing issue, you may make the request under CONTU. Those requests will not count in your five.

Such exceptions need not be logged under CONTU, and CCG compliance may be claimed on the ILL form. Issues older than five years are not governed by CONTU, so CCL is the correct choice on the ILL form.

Other Materials (Including Fiction and Poetry). This applies to materials in books, mostly. Only five copies may be requested from any single work (including collective works) per year, during the entire time a work falls under copyright protection. To illustrate this requirement, imagine there is a book of poetry called *School Days*. Suppose that the school library has an index that lists all the poems in this book and many others. The library doesn't own *School Days*, but teachers use the index to find poems to use with their classes. The public library owns a copy of *School Days* and will supply the school library with photocopies of material from the volume. Four teachers so far this calendar year have requested copies of poems from this work. The school librarian may request one more copy of a poem from this work in this calendar year under the Rule of Five. After that, the school must pay royalties on copies or purchase its own copy of the book. If the librarian places an order for the book, and the copy is not yet received, he or she may request other copies of poems from the book under fair use since the book has been purchased, but not received. This requirement holds true even if the book is out of print. Out-of-print status is not the same as being out of copyright.

Keeping ILL forms on file is the best method of keeping interlibrary loan records. While one must keep the loan records for non-periodical requests for only a calendar year, keeping a history of requests can be helpful for collection development purposes.

Examples and Explanations. (Note: For all these transactions, assume today's date to be June 2, 2000.)

- Patron requests an article from periodical *XYZ*, issue dated December 5, seven years ago. This is the first request for an article from this periodical this year. This request is considered fair use and need not be logged under CONTU because the periodical issue requested is over five years old.

- Patron requests an article from periodical *ABC*, issue dated December 5 three years ago. This is the third request for this periodical this year. This request would be filled under CONTU guidelines and should be logged as request number three on this periodical title.

- Patron requests six poems be copied from a single collective work. No other items have been requested from this collection this year. Only five of the poems may be requested via ILL from this particular title. Perhaps one of the poems could be found in another collection, or the Copyright Clearance Center could be contacted for the cost to reproduce the item. Copies of the ILL request forms for the five permitted reproductions should be retained by the requesting library for one year to track requests per title.

- Patron requests an article from the January 4, 2000, issue of journal *PQR* because the copy is missing from the library's shelves. This request may be filled under CONTU since the requesting library subscribes to the journal. The request does not fall under the Rule of Five, however, because the library owns this title.

- Patron requests an article from the March 15, 2000, issue of journal *NOP*. The library has already requested five articles from this journal from one library this calendar year. Perhaps another library would be a source for five more copies? The requesting library is permitted five requests per calendar year from a single journal title. The library that supplies the requests is not considered in counting the five. All five requests may come from one library, or all five may come from different libraries. The total of five remains the same. This request would fall outside the Rule of Five, and royalties would have to be paid on the sixth request.

Keep in mind that the burden of assuring compliance with the CONTU Guidelines falls on the requesting library (Jackson, p. 87). It is the requesting library that must determine the fair use (CCL) or CONTU (CCG) applicability and also maintain the necessary records. If a request should come into a library, that library may fulfill the request without question since the requesting library will have taken care of the copyright compliance.

Summary. While the CONTU Guidelines may have initially been intended to deal with interlibrary loan, they do provide a conservative set of guidelines for intralibrary loans. And while some stretching of the CONTU limits might be overlooked, beware of anything that might smack of "systematic copying." For more information on copying for interlibrary loan, see this Web site: **www.utsystem.edu/OGC/IntellectualProperty/ l-108g.htm.**

Fax

The latest technology to enter the ILL arena is telefacsimile, commonly known as the fax. While fax simplifies and speeds up interlibrary loan, it complicates copyright compliance. Since most periodicals aren't loose-leaf, the sending library usually must photocopy the required pages before transmitting them via fax. Here's where the problem arises. The relevant section of the copyright law provides for interlibrary loan under the premise that *one* copy be made of the requested information and that the single copy become the property of the patron requesting it. In a fax situation, the sending library creates a photocopy, then faxes it to the requesting library. Now two copies of the information exist—the original photocopy and the fax copy.

While there has been a technical violation of copyright, if the sending library destroys the photocopy when the transmission is complete and confirmed, only one copy exists. Libraries intending to use fax as a means for sending or receiving ILL transactions should be aware of the possible violation of copyright and have written policies and procedures to address the problem (Ensign, p. 126). One certain violation is the plan to keep the original photocopy in a ready-reference collection or vertical file. The first copy of the faxed ILL document *must* be destroyed to comply with the CONTU guidelines.

CONTU Compliance

The CONTU guidelines deal with interlibrary loan of periodical articles and portions of books, and the rules they spell out are very specific. Keep in mind when dealing with these rules that all periodical transactions may not be governed by CONTU.

A simple 3x5 card system such as pictured in Figure 8.1 would provide all the documentation needed for CONTU compliance. A computer database could also maintain the same records. Remember that libraries maintain this type of record only on their requests, not on ILL orders they fill. Whatever record-keeping method you choose, you need to keep records of periodical requests for only four years—the current year plus the three more. Records of requests for materials in books should be kept for four years also, but you need consider only the current year in determining if a particular request exceeds the Rule of Five.

Figure 8.1 *Sample CONTU Card System*

PERIODICAL TITLE					
Year	**Issue**	**Requested**	**Received**	**CCL**	**CCG**

What To Do if You Can't Comply

It was bound to happen. Because of your new CD-ROM periodical index, you have more requests for articles from a certain periodical title than you can legally request under the CONTU Guidelines. What do you do now? You have several options. You can:

- Purchase a subscription to the periodical. Because the law and the guidelines aren't specific about how far back the subscription must go, purchasing a subscription to the current volume has been used as justification for CCG requests for back issues. This is a gray area you will have to wrestle with, assisted by legal counsel.

- Borrow issues from other libraries. Sometimes you have demand only during a particular part of the school year. A public library might lend you its bound volume for a short time. Your patrons can then make their own copies without CONTU implications.

- Advise your patrons of other libraries in the area that either subscribe to the periodical or would make an ILL request.

- Request a copyright-cleared copy of the material from a document delivery service such as University Microfilms or UnCoverWeb. These organizations pay royalties on each copy supplied. But remember that a copy purchased from one of these sources is not cleared for multiple copies, except as under fair use.

- Write to the copyright holder for permission. (See section on permissions for sample forms.)

- Join the Copyright Clearance Center. This organization acts as a clearinghouse for copyright permissions and, while it doesn't supply the articles themselves, it does collect fees for copies and distributes them to copyright holders. (See Chapter 9 on permissions for more information.)

- Purchase back issues from the publisher, if available. Sometimes brokers of back issues can also supply individual issues (Jackson, p. 87).

Summary. Interlibrary loan may not be the panacea to shrinking library budgets. The CONTU guidelines place strict limits on the number of articles a library may request from a periodical title during a calendar year. Articles more than five years old are exempt from the guidelines, but for those covered, a library may request only five articles from a given title during a calendar year. The requesting library must also follow strict record-keeping requirements.

These guidelines help publishers know that they can sell adequate copies of their periodicals to stay profitable. They also assure libraries that their patrons will be able to access infrequently requested periodical titles. CONTU also governs photocopies from books in a similar manner.

While ILL copying between library systems is always governed by CONTU, lending within a system is not. However, the law specifies that "systematic copying" is not acceptable in any circumstance, especially when such copying would take the place of the purchase of materials. The CONTU wording was intended to spell out exactly what "systematic copying" was, so the CONTU guidelines may be considered reasonable limits on ILL requests between schools in the same district.

Reserves

The practice of copying for the purpose of library reserves is becoming more frequent in secondary schools. Not long ago, reserve collections were the domain of university libraries, but as more high schools teach advanced placement and college credit courses, teachers are more likely to assign significant amounts of out-of-class reading. Since the assignments are often from works not likely to be held in the school library, the issue of copying for reserve has entered the secondary library arena.

Copying for reserves wasn't included in the CONTU guidelines or in the fair use guidelines, so several organizations took a stab at defining what was acceptable copying for reserve purposes. The American Library Association's Model Policy Concerning College and University Photocopying for Classroom Research and Library Reserve Use (1982) serves as a framework around which one can formulate local reserve policies. No suits have been brought against schools following these guidelines, so one might presume that these limits are generally accepted.

According to the policy, a faculty member may put his own photocopy (made under the fair use exemption that allows a single copy for personal research) on reserve for students to read. The library can also make a certain number of photocopies of material for reserve use. The amount of material a single teacher can reserve for a course would vary depending on the course, the subject matter, and the difficulty level of the material covered, but it should be "reasonable."

Library reserves, just like multiple photocopies in the classroom, are not to take the place of textbooks or other purchased instructional materials. The purpose should be supplemental, not primary.

The number of copies to be put on reserve should be determined by the library, based on the number of students enrolled in the course. In deciding how many copies to place on reserve, the librarian may consider the difficulty of the material and the amount of time students have to prepare the assignment. He or she must include a notice of copyright on each reserve copy, just as a copyright statement would be marked on any copy made in the library. Photocopying for reserve use should not substitute for the purchase of the work copied, either by the library or by the student. The library should own a copy of the work copied for reserve, but an occasional interlibrary loan or a copy from a faculty member's personal collection is permitted. Such borrowed copying should not be routine, however.

The reserve guidelines also state that copying for reserves should follow the guidelines for classroom use. That policy would indicate that an item photocopied for reserve may not be copied (or retained) for use in a subsequent term without express permission. It also reiterates the need to place a notice of copyright on the first (or only) page of a copy.

Electronic Reserves

Some libraries are trying a new system of putting materials on reserve. Rather than making photocopies of materials, or putting the originals in an area behind the circulation desk, these libraries are scanning the materials and making them available to patrons via a computer network. Making copies electronically is similar to making photocopies as far as reserves are concerned, as long as you can meet the four tests of fair use.

But electronic reserves touch more than just the copying provisions of the law. Each time a user pulls up the image on his screen, a display of the image takes place. If the work has video or audio accompaniment, there is a performance. Sending the image over the computer network is a transmission. There is no case law to guide us here. If you plan to provide remote (e.g. from home) access to works, especially multimedia works, you would be well advised to seek permission for such access. There is little protection in the law for such uses (University of Texas System, 1996).

The Conference on Fair Use (CONFU) has collaboratively worked out a draft of a system of guidelines for electronic reserves (Electronic Reserves Drafting Sub-Group, 1996). These guidelines have still not been approved as of this writing, but the limits detailed here may be within acceptable limits for such uses. The guidelines as proposed cover only copyrighted materials, and do not include materials for which libraries have other license agreements in place, such as full-text periodical databases. Note that many publishers have expressed strong objections to electronic reserves, and there may be significant modification to these rules before a final agreement is reached, (if ever).

As a rule of thumb, copy or scan only short items into electronic reserve systems: short journal articles, book chapters, or a poem from a collection. Longer items should be excerpted. "Short" is defined as items of customary length as long as they are a small part of the whole work. The instructor must request the items to be placed on reserve; the library may not make the decision about what to place on reserve. Items in the electronic reserve system must be taken from legal copies owned by the instructor, the library, or some other unit of the institution. And finally, the amount of material placed on reserve must be a small portion of the total amount of assigned reading.

Additional requirements proposed in this preliminary draft include a prominent notice of copyright and a caution against further distribution of the item. Access restrictions are also a part of the proposed guidelines, which suggest that only students enrolled in the course for which the items are reserved should be able to access the materials, and they should not have to pay to access them.

Just as with paper copies, items may not be re-used from term to term without express permission of the copyright holder.

For more information on electronic reserves, see these two Web sites: **<www.cc.columbia.edu/~rosedale/guidelines.html>** and **www.utsystem.edu/ OGC/IntellectualProperty/l-resele.htm.**

Chapter 9

Permissions: Copyright vs. Contract

T he central theme of this book is "if uncertain, ask permission." That sounds simple enough. The difficulty comes first in deciding when to ask permission, and second in knowing how to ask permission.

As discussed in the chapter on fair use, for some applications written permission is not necessary. Fair use guidelines are explicit regarding the instances for which educators need not seek permission. Some of the highly specific fair use guidelines are, effectively, permission in advance as long as certain requirements are met. For print works, the rules detailed in Chapter 3 on print materials determine if copies can be considered fair use. For audiovisuals, if the use meets all of the five fair use criteria, permission is granted automatically:

■ The performance occurs in a nonprofit educational institution; and

■ The performance is used for face-to-face teaching; and

■ The performance is presented by instructors or pupils; and

■ The performance takes place in a classroom or similar place for instruction (including the library); and

■ The performance is of a legally acquired (or legally copied) copy of the work.

More detailed descriptions of the fair use guidelines are given in the chapters covering various types of materials.

Some materials are covered by copyright but, for a particular reason, the copyright holder has decided to withhold rights for the work. In such an instance the copyright holder will license the work rather than sell it. This practice is quite common in the computer software area, where publishers wish licensees to have very specific, restricted rights.

Copyright law allows a copyright holder to modify the blanket copyright provisions via contract. In essence, that means that you may sign your fair use rights away and not even know it if you send in a product registration card or license agreement or even fill out an order blank without reading the fine print. It is possible to modify the license or contract by simply marking out and initialing the portions of the license agreement or order form conditions that you wish to change, when you send it in. The copyright owner may or may not agree to your modifications. If the owner refuses to accept your modifications, you may either reconsider your position or elect to purchase other materials that you may license or purchase with the rights you require.

Several years ago some innovative software publishers tried to sneak this little-noticed feature of the law past the buying public via so-called "shrink-wrap" licenses. The main thrust of the shrink-wrap license was to bind the purchaser to a lengthy and technical set of license restrictions in a negative fashion. The purchaser was to read the provisions of the contract in super-fine print through the shrink-wrap on the package, for once the shrink-wrap was broken, the purchaser would be bound by the contract provisions. Some of the restrictions could be extreme; they included a prohibition against disposing of the software and, in the case of libraries, a prohibition against lending the software. Many licenses conveyed usage rights only; the software itself remained the property of the copyright holder.

Consumers were outraged. Several consumer protection agencies tackled the problem, even taking the shrink-wrap contract to several court challenges. Results varied from state to state. Some upheld the copyright owner's right to limit the sale of rights with the software; others ruled the contract null and void. Check with experts in your own state to see what rights bind you in software shrink-wrap contracts.

While shrink-wrap licenses and publishers' restrictive statements may seem discouraging, the good news is that the "home use only" stickers often found on videos are not binding on schools in any way, unless a statement agreeing to such use is part of the purchase contract. This unfortunate bit of wording serves to explain only that this particular copy of the video does not come with public performance rights. Public performance rights are not required for qualifying curricular performances, so home-use-only tapes may be used in instructional situations. Home-use-only videos *may not* be used for reward, entertainment, or time-filling situations without permission or royalty payment.

Rental videos may be restricted to home use only if the membership agreement you signed when you got the video membership specified that there were to be no public performances of the films rented from the video store. In such a case, permission is required—not from the copyright holder, since performance in a school is permissible under fair use—but from the video store! This is a contract problem, not a copyright issue. Few video stores make customers sign rental agreements any more, so this issue is mostly moot.

Nonprofit Commercial Activities

Schools, while being nonprofit organizations, often partake in a bit of fund raising. Video and audio are a favorite form of money-making. Booster clubs often sell tapes (audio or video) of athletic or band performances; drama clubs may offer a video of the class play; the journalism class may put together a video yearbook; PTA may offer parents videos of their children in the spring field day. Any or all of these may have music to accompany the action. Unfortunately, some copyright liabilities apply. Carol Ruth Shepherd remarked in the Internet newsgroup CNI-Copyright that in order to sell videotapes, organizations must get permission from the persons in the performance, get performance and distribution rights for any musical or dramatic works included, and get sync rights for any music used to accompany the program (Shepherd, May 24, 1996).

Permissions

After checking all the angles, you've discovered that your anticipated use of some material will not be considered fair use. You know you will need permission from the copyright holder to reproduce or use the desired material. How do you obtain this permission? What information will the copyright holder want from you? How much will it cost? How do you even find out who owns the copyright so you can ask them? Good questions, all.

There are several points to keep in mind when requesting permissions, no matter if the request is for print, video, or any other copyrighted material.

- Make your request far enough in advance that the copyright owner has a reasonable chance to respond. A month in advance should be sufficient, but six weeks is better for print materials. For information from the Internet, a week's notice is usually sufficient for a first-time classroom use. For nonclassroom use or repeat use, consider that the owner might be on vacation and cannot respond to your electronic request right away. Allow at least a month.

- Be specific in your request. Don't say, "Please grant all rights to . . . ." You'll be turned down. Try to be exact: "I would like to request archival rights to XYZ videotape," or "I would like to photocopy pages 4 and 5 of your book for a workshop I will be teaching" are much more likely to receive a favorable response.

- Don't be surprised if there is a fee for the rights you request. Authors and producers make their living selling their products. By making copies, you are using their material without paying for a new copy. They may decide to charge a fee for the permission you request, and they are within their rights to do so. You are free to decline to pay for the permission, but in that case you may not use the material.

Tracking down the copyright owner to ask permission may be the major hurdle. For works created prior to 1978, most copyrighted materials have some indication of copyright ownership, though sometimes that person or company may not be easy to find. For works created after January 1, 1978, all works are to be considered copyrighted unless proved otherwise. Finding out who owns these copyrights may be a frustrating procedure.

Make sure you send your request to the correct person. While the author owned the copyright at the moment the work was created, it is unlikely that the author still owns the copyright in published works. Check the back of the title page for the name of the copyright holder. If the holder is a publisher, the address can be found in *Books in Print*, *The Literary Marketplace*, or one of several directories of the publishing industry.

Be aware that some materials incorporated in copyrighted works are quoted with permission of the original copyright holder. Such uses are acknowledged in a section on the same page as the copyright information. If the work you want permission to use incorporates parts of other works, you must get separate permissions from each of those second-tier copyright holders.

If the permission you are requesting is urgent and essential, telephone the publisher to make sure you have the correct address and contact person to whom to send the request. Such seemingly minor information can smooth an otherwise lengthy process.

Fortunately, the Library of Congress Office of Copyright maintains records of registered copyrights. Those seeking copyright information can go to the library and perform their own searches through the copyright records or pay the library an hourly fee to perform searches for them. Additionally, copyright records are available online through the Library of Congress LOCIS online information system at **<lcWeb.loc.gov/copyright/>**. Just remember that a work need not be registered to be copyrighted. The fact that you don't find a registration in the LOCIS system does not mean the work is unprotected. It may mean you should look for a work whose copyright owner is more accessible.

When writing a letter requesting permission to reproduce or use copyrighted information, keep in mind that you may be addressing this letter to the permissions department of a publishing house. This staff may have to deal with hundreds of titles. To speed your permission approval, help the staff as much as possible by being specific in your request. Include these items in your permission letter:

- Author or editor, title, and edition of the material.

- Exact description of the material to be used or copied, including amount, page numbers, scenes or footage, chapters, any other locator information. In the case of print works, include a photocopy of the material under consideration.

- The number of copies to be made.

- Purpose of the copies.

- How the material will be distributed or used (in class, closed circuit, modified for a mural, placed in a newsletter).

- Cost of the material, if any.

- How material will be reproduced, if copied (photocopy, ditto, photographic enlargement, archival copy, or other).

In a work with included copyright information, you may find multiple copyright dates, and you may find a long list of acknowledgments. Any material covered in the acknowledgments section of the copyright information is covered by separate copyrights. The copyright holder of the primary work cannot grant permission to reproduce material under another's copyright. You will need to apply directly to those rights holders.

If your first inclination is to send your request for permission to the person or firm from which you purchased the material, ignore it. This tendency is especially prevalent in the case of video permissions. Distributors may have been designated by the copyright holder as agents who can grant permissions, but this is not generally the case. There are several agencies that do nothing but broker permissions. The Motion Picture Licensing Corporation and Movie Licensing USA handle many of the film and video permissions. ASCAP, BMI, and Harry Fox Agency broker an assortment of music licenses.

The Copyright Clearance Center (CCC) offers several types of print permission services. CCC was established after Congress suggested a mechanism be created to facilitate compliance with print reproduction rights, as defined by the copyright law of 1976. CCC is the Reproduction Rights Organization (RRO) for the United States. Other countries have similar organizations. Rights holders register their works with CCC and set the royalty fees that CCC collects on their behalf. Users report and pay for their copying either through a license or each time they use a registered work.

CCC offers a number of services, several of which are useful for schools:

- The Transactional Reporting Service (TRS) provides users with immediate authorization to make photocopies from over 1.75 million publications. By using CCC, educators do not have to make individual fee payments to publishers, but instead pay a combined fee to CCC, which distributes it to copyright owners. This service would be useful for duplication of nonacademic materials such as parenting resources, counseling information, and community education materials.

- The Academic Permissions Service (APS) enables a school to clear documents for academic course packs and classroom handouts. The APS provides customers with a catalog of all CCC-registered titles and royalty fees. In addition, CCC will seek permission for many titles not covered by pre-authorized agreements. Permissions can be received in as little as 48 hours. This service will be useful for reproduction of documents for which fair use is not an option, such as repeated copying beyond the first term.

- The Electronic Course Content Service (ECCS) is similar to APS but applies to materials used in electronic format, such as online courses, electronic reserves, and electronic handouts.

As well as offering these services, CCC has specialized services for several kinds of reproduction and distribution rights. For more information, contact the Copyright Clearance Center at **<www.copyright.com>**.

The Colorado Alliance of Research Libraries UnCoverWeb offers access to and delivery of millions of articles from thousands of periodical titles. Each article has been copyright-cleared for individual use. Permission is still needed for non-fair-use applications. While it is possible to order articles via mail and phone, the fastest form of delivery is through a computer connection to the Internet. As of this writing, UnCoverWeb may be reached by using a Web browser to access **<uncWeb.carl.org/>**. UnCoverWeb will fax copyright-cleared articles, usually within 24 hours; one-hour service is available. Coverage is mostly of academic journals—not typical high school fare—but for those with specific needs, this is a rapid source.

If you decide to request permission directly from the copyright owner or publisher, Figures 9.1 and 9.2 will provide a simple, fill-in-the-blanks option. It is not applicable to all situations, but it will cover most requests for print permissions.

On receipt of a permission request such as this, publishers have three options:

Figure 9.1

Request for Permission

Permissions Department   Date:_____

Dear Reader:

This letter is a request for permission to duplicate/use for

_____, the following:

Title:_____

Copyright:_____

Author(s):_____

Material to be duplicated:_____

Number of copies:_____

Manner of distribution:_____

Type of reproduction:_____

Purpose of use/reproduction:_____

A self-addressed, stamped envelope is enclosed for your convenience. Please respond and notify me of fees, if any, for this permission.

Sincerely,

Name_____

School name_____

School address_____

City, ST ZIP_____

                                Permission granted_____

                                Date_____

                                Conditions, if any_____

                                             _____

                                             _____

                                             _____

- They can approve your request as stated. In that instance you will likely receive your letter back, stamped "approved."

- They may state the terms under which the copyright holder will grant your permission and ask you to sign the attached agreement and perhaps include payment of a stated fee.

- They may decline your request. Remember, this is their property. They need not offer any reason for refusal.

Figure 9.2

Sample Request for Permission

Permissions Department   Date: **9 September 1993**

Dear Reader:

This letter is a request for permission to duplicate/use for

next semester, the following:

Title: **Practical copyright for schools**

Copyright: **Company name, 1978, 1980, 1991**

Author(s): **J. Jones**

Material to be duplicated: **Pages 35, 36 and 37 in Chapter one.**

See enclosed photocopies

Number of copies: **143 (1 per student in 5 classes)**

Manner of distribution: **There will be no charge for the materials**

Type of reproduction: **ditto**

Purpose of use/reproduction: **Library orientation for freshmen**

A self-addressed, stamped envelope is enclosed for your convenience. Please respond and notify me of fees, if any, for this permission.

Sincerely,

Name_____

School name_____

School address_____

City, ST ZIP_____

Permission granted_____

Date_____

Conditions, if any_____

_____

_____

If you receive permission to use certain material in exchange for some form of payment, and you later elect *not* to use the material, be sure to notify the agency from which you received the permission. In some instances you will be expected to pay the fee unless you notify the rights holder that the use will not take place. These rights brokers assume the use unless they are notified.

You may never hear anything at all from your request. *No response does not equal no objection.* There could have been any number of things that prevented the owner from responding, including the fact that she never received your request. Remember that copyright transfers, permissions, and the like must be in writing. You may hear the suggestion to word your permission request like this: "If I don't hear from you by such-and-such date, I will assume I have permission to … " Such wording is not recommended. The copyright owner is not required to respond to requests, and the lack of response is not to be construed as permission.

Student and Parent Permissions

Publishers aren't the only ones who hold copyrights. Your students own the copyrights on their own works. Before you publish original student work, or reproduce it for a workshop or competition, or display it in a gallery, mall, Web site, or other public place, you will need permission from the student or his parents. Appendix F provides an example of the type of permission a school or teacher would require to make use of student work. Displaying work in the classroom would likely not require such permission since that use involves students and teachers in the class. Public use beyond the classroom would require permission.

Keep in mind that if a student is a minor, parental approval is required. Make the request for permission specific, in the manner of a request to a publisher. A parent would want to know how the child will be identified with the work, to whom the work will be displayed, and for how long. Don't request or expect blanket permission to be granted for all classroom work. While such a request is easy, it would probably be entirely too vague to be enforceable.

Summary

- Apply for permission early to allow sufficient time for permission to arrive.

- Send your permission request to the correct party. If in doubt, research through Library of Congress Copyright Office.

- Take advantage of rights brokers. They can simplify and streamline permissions.

- Be specific in describing the material and the rights you seek.

- If you do not use an item for which a fee or conditions of use were required, notify the correct agency. Otherwise you may be held responsible for fees, since use may be assumed.

Chapter *10*

Copyright and the Internet

Suppose you write a document on a word processor. Perhaps it is a poem or a chapter of a book. As soon as you save the file on the hard disk, your work is protected under copyright. You can send the chapter to your publisher, you can ask other writers to read the manuscript and give suggestions, and you can pass out copies at workshops. The work is still protected under copyright law. Should one of those people take your manuscript and misuse it, you could sue with a reasonable likelihood of success. You may register your work with the copyright office if you like, but registration isn't required. Registration does, however, confer a number of important advantages for enforcement.

Now suppose you put that very same manuscript on your Internet home page. Have you just abandoned the copyright to that work? Not at all. You still own all six rights of a copyright holder: reproduction, distribution, adaptation, public performance, public display, and digital audio transmission. And so does every other creator of materials available via the Internet.

Every creator? Yes. Every person who writes a document published on the Internet, who creates a graphic or icon, who scans his own photograph or records his own voice into a digital file, who sends an electronic mail message, who creates a document for a newsgroup, or who designs a Web page owns the copyright to his creative work. And because the United States is a signatory to the Berne Convention, no notice of copyright is required on *any* item in order for the item to be protected by copyright law.

As the creator, that person can decide exactly how he wishes that material to be used. Obviously the creator has decided to permit display of this work via the

Internet since he included it on a Web page, sent it via e-mail, or posted it to a newsgroup. The fact that the copyright holder elected to share his work in this manner, however, does not mean that anyone can freely appropriate that material for other uses.

As a friend likes to point out, "There is a difference between 'can't' and 'not supposed to.'" The technology exists for someone to view a document or graphic and, by clicking on the appropriate button or menu, grab that item in a pure digital form. From that point it is quite simple to adapt, modify, resend, forward, copy, or display the item. Someone could certainly do those things, but one is not supposed to. Why not? Because the rights to do all those things are reserved for the copyright holder. All the copyright holder permits when an item is displayed on the Internet is to allow you to view the item as you navigate around the network (Bender, p. 1).

Certainly there are some documents that state they have been dedicated to the public domain, or that use for nonprofit purposes is permitted by the copyright holder. Naturally these situations are apart from the average item located on the Internet. And a case may be made for "fair use" of Internet materials, just as one may make a claim of fair use for print and audiovisual materials. Similar situations must apply before a claim of fair use may be considered valid. Since there are to this point virtually no significant cases dealing with fair use of Internet materials, one must analyze and evaluate every use in the light of the general guidelines. Remember that each of the four tests of fair use must be weighed against every claim:

- *The purpose of the use.* Is it for nonprofit educational purposes? Displaying a Web page or making a transparency of some information for the purposes of teaching a lesson at a public or nonprofit private school would likely be looked upon favorably.

- *The character of the use.* What type of material is going to be used? Factual material placed on the Internet has little protection of copyright since facts can't be copyrighted. If you are using lists of common facts such as the 10 longest rivers, or population figures, you have much more latitude to use the material. Highly creative material, such as artwork, videos, or Web page design would be much more highly protected.

- *The amount of material copied (also called the extent).* How much of the material are you going to use? If you plan to copy the entire item (whole text file, complete graphic, entire Web page) you'd best have good answers to the other three qualifying questions. The more of an item you plan to use, the less leeway you are permitted. This factor has significant impact on software that can capture entire Web sites for use in an offline situation.

- *The effect of the use on the market for the work.* What effect would your type of use have if everyone made similar use of the material? For example, if everyone were to download the whole Web page, do you think anyone would want to visit the site? Probably not. Some sites have advertising or other agendas; their authors want users to see those friendly notices. By downloading the page to an offline machine, you would miss the constantly changing variety of advertisements that the sponsor of the page spends lots of money for you to see. Missing those advertisements would potentially deprive the sponsor of revenue. As far as copyright goes, that is a no-no.

What if the page is put up by a nonprofit individual or organization? The same reasoning applies:

- Perhaps the author of the document will one day develop that information into a book or magazine article. Would the market for the book be as great if everyone were to capture the material from the Internet?

- Maybe the nonprofit organization wants Internet explorers to see the wealth of material its members can assemble; if you capture a document you'd have little reason to return to this site.

- Or the information is quickly dated and the organization feels it would be harmed if it were identified with outdated material.

There are many ways that downloading Internet material can wreak financial harm on the copyright holder.

Keep in mind that each classroom use of material retrieved from the Internet must be weighed against the four factors listed earlier in this chapter and several other places in this book. Imagine a scale; each of the four factors weighs either for you or against you, and the fourth factor weighs much more than all the others. Consider that when making your analysis.

OSP Liability

The Digital Millennium Copyright Act established some forms of protection from liability that may affect schools. Detailed in Section 512, the many specific requirements to be eligible for protection under this section are quite complex. Essentially, the law states that if an Internet (or online) service provider (ISP or OSP) registers with the copyright office, and if he agrees to a set of conditions—for instance, to remove potentially infringing materials once they are brought to his attention—the copyright infringement of the OSP is limited. This protection extends only to the school or district, not to the individuals who may have committed the infringements. The designation of someone to be the copyright agent for notification of claims of copyright infringement is one step that schools can easily take. A single person who will respond to claims of copyright infringement is designated by the school and registered with the copyright office **<lcWeb.loc.gov/copyright/onlinesp/>**. Complete contact information for this person should be found on the school Web site. If someone should find contraband material on a Web page, the copyright agent is notified, who then takes down or disables access to the material in question.

Use of Electronic Mail

The author of an e-mail message owns the content of that message. You as the recipient may not make copies of that message or distribute it without the consent of the original author. This holds true for messages you may forward to third parties without the express consent of the original author. There would probably be allowances to reprint some or all of the message in a reply to the sender. You might also paraphrase the message in the reply. Since you are sending that information back to the copyright holder, there would likely be no problem.

One of the critical questions asked in determining if a use of a copyrighted work is fair is "Has the work been published?" Typically, private e-mail has never been published in such a way that many people would be likely to have seen it. Since the work has not been published, it is unlikely that the work could ever fall into a situation covered by fair use (Cyberspace Law Institute, 1996). In addition, if the e-mail is created at work under the scope of employment, there is the possibility that the e-mail is a work for hire. Are there any court cases to support this? Not yet.

For safety parameters, keep private e-mail private unless you have express permission of the original writer. Don't forward it to newsgroups or listservs, don't include it in a message to a third party, and don't post it on your Web page, unless you have permission. It's good manners; it's good practice.

Use of Newsgroup and Discussion List Information

When someone posts a message to a newsgroup or a discussion list, she makes an implied decision to "publish" the work. Once a work is published, there is much more latitude to use portions of that work within the fair use exemption. The author may, however, negate that implied license simply by noting in the posting that she requests the material not be distributed beyond the list. Again, there are no significant court cases to support these assumptions. These are rules derived from the world of print and extrapolated into cyberspace.

As a guideline, you can probably copy a few sentences or paragraphs of a newsgroup or discussion list posting since it was published, as long as you aren't going to use it for a money-making purpose. You can also probably repost the article or message to another newsgroup unless the original author states that isn't permitted. It is always good manners (and safe legal practice) to ask permission to repost.

Use of Web Page Information

When deciding how to use a Web page, consider the same factors you would for a print document or an audiovisual item (depending on what you will be using from the Web.) Keep in mind the four tests of fair use. The nonprofit educational use is a given, but what about the character and extent of the material used? The more creative the site (i.e., the less factual), the less of it may be used without permission. As a matter of good teaching, one would want to make the best use of

Q: *Must I have permission to put a link to another Web page on my own page?*

A: Links have been likened to cross references in a library card catalog. They are facts (just like street addresses) and cannot be protected by copyright, so making links should be acceptable. Some sites don't like you to "deep link" (linking deeper into the site than the main page) because you might miss advertising there. These sites may object, but it shouldn't be on copyright grounds. If you use frames, remember that the referred site will appear to be on your server. Some sites may object to the implied relationship.

Q: *I print out pages from the Internet, photocopy them, and pass them along to my department heads. I usually include notes for them to "share" this with members of their department. Can I legally print out pages from the Internet by invoking the browser print function?*

A: Under fair use you may make a *single* copy of up to a chapter of a book or an article of a magazine (not the entire work) for you own *personal* use and education, including use in teaching.

These teachers aren't your students so they don't qualify for the fair use exemption. (If they were your students, you would have some limited ability to make multiple copies.) You will need permission to make the copies you describe.

teaching resources. One doesn't use more of a video than is necessary to make a point. Teaching time is too valuable. So one would make optimum use of Web-based resources, as well. Use what is necessary, then get on to other things.

Using any Web page involves a display of the material. Display is the right of the copyright holder. While a display to an individual is expected, display to a public group (your class) isn't. Material located shortly before use, before permission could normally be expected—say a week before anticipated use, since most Webmasters can be reached electronically—could be used for a single lesson. Beyond that use, request permission. Any repeat use *always* needs permission, whether this re-use is in the same term or in subsequent terms.

Beware of programs that allow you to capture an entire Web site or portion of a site for use offline. While this is a boon to teachers with unreliable Web connections, downloading and storing Web pages or sites for public display in a classroom involves several problems. The author(s) and copyright holders design Web pages to be interactive and responsive. Many have ever-changing sponsorships and real-time data that is designed to be viewed in an active, not a static, environment. The owners of these sites have the authority to decide if they feel that your proposed collection of their work fits into their plans. Remember that under the fair use tests, one of the significant questions is how much of the item will be used. If one captures the entire site, one is taking 100 percent. Since Web pages are ordinarily highly creative in design and content (the character of the use), the likelihood for a ruling of fair use declines significantly.

In a discussion of this topic on the Internet newsgroup LM_NET, Stephen Collins, Webmaster of Web66, commented:

> Not only is [copying Web pages] very probably a violation of copyright law, it is certainly unethical, and to your students it models a lack of respect for other people's property. It also has very concrete consequences. I run Web66, which is funded by grant monies and by the University of Minnesota. They provide funding in large part based on the popularity of Web66. If I can show only a few accesses because you've all [duplicated] your own copies, then I won't be able to get funding to continue Web66. If you all access it directly, and I can show that it gets 40,000 hits per day from 2,000 different organizations and 25 different countries, then I won't have any trouble getting funding. Most "free" sites are in the same position. When you [copy] them, you're killing off your own resources.

He makes a powerful argument, which reinforces the old saying "There ain't no free lunch."

In creating Web pages, you need to be concerned about using copyrighted materials on those pages. You must make copies to put a page on the Web, and frequently you must also convert materials from an analog format to digital to get the information on the Internet. Music, multimedia elements, and other copyrighted information, once mounted on a Web page, are not only copied but distributed and performed publicly. All these conditions are cause for concern. In the interest of copyright compliance, some rights brokers have established a "click-through" license for quick, efficient licensing (ASCAP, BMI). Note that there is no automatic fair use for these types of elements on Web pages. Each individual use must be subjected to a fair use analysis.

Chat

Chat is as spontaneous as face-to-face conversation. However, few people record (or "fix") conversation. There is no case law regarding the ownership of chat conversations. Extrapolating from other media, one might be able to say that chat is ephemeral, not "fixed." No copyright is vested in a communication that is not fixed in a tangible medium of expression. If the chat is captured, however, fixation automatically generates a copyright for the author of each communication. So each "send" might be construed as a separate "work" protected by copyright, or a series of posts might be taken as a long, possibly disjointed, document.

Copying Internet Code

While it is possible to download a site's HTML code and incorporate the design into your own page, remember that the creative work that went into the design is also copyrighted. Just as copying a drawing or painting requires permission, if you admire the design work of a Web page, ask the creator before you appropriate the result.

Summary

Web-based material is copyrighted just as print and audiovisual materials are, and notification of copyright status is not required. Small portions of Web documents may be used by teachers in class if there is not sufficient time to secure permission, just as with print materials. Large chunks of images, documents, and Web sites should not be taken without prior consent. Watch for Web pages granting permission for use in educational situations. There are many.

Since there is greater latitude for student use of copyrighted materials, they may also use modest portions of Web documents as long as the copies they make belong to them. Teachers may not keep copies or originals of works made by students in which they incorporate materials copied from the Internet. The copies made from the Internet must reside with the student.

Remember that showing a Web document to a class constitutes a public performance or display of that page. Copyright law and its associated guidelines don't speak of the Internet, but common sense can gauge how closely a given use meets the fair use test. And, as always, permission can override any limitations imposed by the law or guidelines. The good news is that the persons responsible for many Web pages have e-mail links built right into the pages, so contacting the proper party for permission is a lot simpler than tracking down print or video copyright holders.

When putting up your own Web page, make sure you have the proper rights for the graphics, designs, logos, and photos you use. Photos are especially touchy. You need permission not only from the photographer, but also from any recognizable person in the photograph. When requesting permission, as in all permission cases, verify that you are getting rights from the person authorized to grant such rights.

Chapter 11

Managing Copyright in Schools

K nowing the rules that govern copyright is only the tip of the copyright management iceberg when one considers the difficulty of explaining to complacent faculty and administrators that they may be at risk if they continue current practices. The person who shatters the long-held belief in free use of all materials for educational purposes can expect to be met with anger, disbelief, or outright hostility.

The library media specialist is the person in any school building most likely to have had some training in copyright. Because the librarian is aware of the risks and sees all aspects of school practice, he is the one most apt to broach the subject of infringement. He is also at highest risk of noncompliance because much of the infringement-prone equipment is run through the library; computer networks, media distribution systems, and overhead and opaque projectors in many cases tie back to the library. If he might be the mostly likely to know that this equipment is being used to violate copyright, the librarian could be named in a copyright infringement action. In a "sue-'em-all" scenario, this is a common practice.

Some librarians take it upon themselves to be the "copyright police," thinking that they are protecting themselves from danger and their schools from legal action. While this is a noble intent, a librarian acting alone in this capacity will probably alienate the faculty with overzealous enforcement. Since he must maintain a collegial relationship with the faculty in order for them to support a schoolwide information literacy program, he'd be more effective as a consultant in a school-wide copyright management program. As the instructional and administrative leader in a building, the principal is best suited to head up the copyright enforcement effort.

The person who is most at risk in a single school situation is the administrative leader–the principal. In virtually any copyright action against a single building, the principal is most likely to be named as a party to the case. As the instructional leader, the principal is responsible for all activities that occur under her purview, so getting the librarian on board a copyright management program is essential for the building and himself.

Managing copyright in a building really begins at the district level. When districts are cited for copyright infractions, one of the first things they are required to do in reparation is to write and adopt a district copyright policy. A district policy establishes an administrative expectation of copyright compliance on the part of employees and students. Interestingly, employees seem to have more trepidation of violating district policy than they do of violating federal law. A clear, board-approved policy, with supporting staff development, can go a long way to achieving maximum copyright compliance in a district. Chapter 13 and Appendix E provide examples and rationale for a strong copyright policy statement. For a building level person to gain cooperation for a serious copyright compliance effort, a district-level policy is the best start.

Beyond a policy, there are other issues to be dealt with in managing copyright. Both things and people require some degree of modification if a copyright compliance effort is to succeed. By working to mitigate both human and inanimate aspects of the problem, the administrator, librarian, technology specialist or other copyright officer can reduce (though likely never eliminate) copyright infringements and still maintain collegial relationships.

Managing Things

Managing things is a good place to begin because it is easy, and things don't complain. Having all your inanimate objects properly prepared for copyright compliance will also ease the people who must deal with the things into compliance. For those who are new to an understanding of their obligations under copyright law, overt and repeated notices will help remind them that each item has a copyright consideration. While the people may not like to see them, the notices are less objectionable than a nagging voice or wagging finger; they are constant, they are visible, they are explicit. In short, preparing all the things prepares you to prepare the people. Each type of thing has its own special management requirements.

Print

- Books generally have copyright information printed on the back of the title page.

- Magazines usually list copyright information on the masthead page. Making copyright control notations in the catalog record (MARC tag 540) or on the protective cover for each title will aid inquiries.

- Plays are controlled under the print guidelines, but the most common abuse of the copyright of plays is performance of all or part of the play to a public audience. Keep a record of any performance rights purchased with the scripts (either in the library or the department in which the play resides). Maintain these records as long as the scripts are held in the district.

■ Poetry is also controlled by the print guidelines. Watch the back of the title page for copyright control information. Many collections combine copyright-protected materials from many sources. Know who is the copyright owner of the materials you use.

■ Images are also protected under the print or multimedia guidelines. Individual images usually have some notice of copyright attached to the print, or listed in the credits section if published in book form. Public display of images on Web pages is a potential problem of which to be aware.

Video and Film

■ Video will require tracking both incoming and outgoing. Know what performance rights were purchased with the tape. Public performance rights are required for noncurricular showings. Stickers on the tapes themselves make public performance tapes easy for browsers to identify when they need a video right away for rainy-day recess or fill-in for a teacher who must attend a conference or leave school unexpectedly. (Purchase copyright compliance stickers from library or office supply houses, or from Sudanco 800-926-0139).

■ Off-air videotapes made in-house should have a prominent notice stating the expiration date of off-air rights (which may vary anywhere from the standard 10/45-day period to life-of-tape rights granted by certain producers to educational users).

■ Any off-air tapes brought in from students or teachers should have a certification of eligibility signed before use. Prepare this form in advance and have it handy. (See p. 59)

Audio, Including Music

■ Audio requirements are similar to video. Using music as background for multimedia productions will likely be the largest demand. Playing audio in public performances such as graduations, dances, and school news broadcasts may be problematic. Providing a collection of royalty-free music clips and links to royalty-free clip sites on the Internet are ways to make compliance easier. (See Appendix C)

Computer Software

■ For software that is checked out of libraries, specific copyright notice is required. Stickers to notify borrowers of their copyright obligations are available from the suppliers listed in Appendix C. If the library is alerted that a patron plans to violate copyright, the library staff should remind the patron of his copyright responsibilities. If he still indicates plans to violate copyright, they should refuse the loan.

- Home software that is installed on school computers should "live" at school. The box, documentation, or license should be at the computer where the software is installed. The home is unlikely to be audited; the school is much more at risk.

- Retain license documents and purchase orders of all school-owned software, including operating systems. Retain the base license when software is upgraded, since often the upgrade license doesn't qualify as a base license. This is especially true for upgraded operating systems. If you owned DOS computers that were upgraded to Windows, you must have both a license for DOS and a license for the Windows upgrade. Machines that started with Windows will have a complete Windows license, not an upgrade license. Cases have been reported in the press of schools sued for software copyright infringement because they couldn't produce either the base license or purchase orders for old operating systems on an audit.

Hardware

Many common pieces of AV hardware in a school are capable of being used to violate copyright. Just as unattended copy machines must have copyright notices attached to protect the host library, placing prominent notices on other machines with infringement potential is a good plan. Consider notices for computers, overhead projectors, VCRs, opaque projectors, CD burners, and cassette recorders.

Local Area Network Resources

Networked software also requires monitoring. License tracking is available through networking software and third party products. A low-tech solution to monitoring license agreements is to use the networking software to control access to networked programs and resources. Set up network logins as the application itself (e.g. "word") and allow only these logins to access the necessary files to run the program. Set the number of simultaneous logins for that login name to the number of licenses you have for the program. You can easily control the number of people who can access a given program because the network software will not allow more people to log in to that account than you have established.

Internet

Interpret fair use item by item using the existing guidelines. Include copyright compliance in acceptable use policies, and make information about copyright part of all Internet training. Internet is a danger spot in copyright compliance because so much material is mounted on the Web in violation of copyright. Just because something is on the Web doesn't mean it is free for use or is mounted with permission.

Managing People

Dealing with the human factor will be the largest problem in achieving copyright compliance. Most teachers will not like a change in copyright enforcement. Some of them have been operating under the "if it's for educational use it's okay" assumption for many years. The person who tells them that their common, convenient practice is a copyright violation is apt to be met with hostility. Help them accept the change by having materials on hand to simplify record keeping. Offer public domain or royalty-free materials to fill in for infringing uses of protected materials. A few materials with public performance rights are always useful for those stressful times when a teacher must leave unexpectedly and an aide fills in until a substitute can arrive.

Public domain materials or materials with performance rights are also useful for time-fillers (waiting for the bus, rainy-day recess) and reward situations (perfect attendance, achievement of academic goals) The cost of public performance rights pales in comparison to the cost of a lawsuit. Many materials come with public performance rights. Ask vendors, or see Appendix K for a list of suppliers who offer public performance rights with their wares.

Here are some tips on dealing with the human factor in copyright compliance:

Students

Students, in their short excerpts in papers and incorporation of minor images in artwork or collages, haven't been significant copyright risks for schools. New multimedia guidelines and the ability for students to publish widely on the Internet have made student use of copyright-protected materials a new area of concern.

The new multimedia guidelines in the United States require that *all* multimedia presentations using copyrighted materials adhere to a set of recommendations that include opening screens that carry notice of copyrighted content, and credit pages listing complete copyright ownership information for each item used under fair use. When students are taught this procedure from an early age, documentation can simply become part of the creative process. Since wording of notices isn't specified in the guidelines, these notices can be put in terms that even second graders can understand.

Teachers

For many years the teacher has been able to use, without challenge, whatever materials she felt necessary or convenient. Disabusing the faculty of these notions is a monumental task. As the instructional leader of a building, the building administrator needs to take a leadership role in guiding the faculty to a new understanding of their obligations regarding copyright. This guidance can be as simple as a directive, "We will abide by all laws that affect our work."

A better approach is to encourage faculty to move toward copyright compliance, with the administration taking extra pains to ensure that they model the behaviors they expect from the faculty.

One technique that has worked well for many schools on the road to copyright compliance is to clear all video with the principal. This process, while painful to some, is likely to bring copyright to the forefront of discussion. One elementary school, after a vivid copyright workshop, chose to enforce appropriate use of video as their first step toward copyright compliance. All video shown in classrooms had to be pre-approved by the principal to verify legitimate tie-in to the curriculum of the grade level and subject.

At the end of the first school year of compliance, the librarian reported that video usage had declined by 75 percent! Incidentally, test scores also rose in that building that year, though there had been no changes in curriculum or methodology. While no attempt was made to tie the rise in test scores to the reduction of noncompliant video, consider that if one tallied up all the entertainment and reward video shown in school, and applied that time to curricular instruction, how much content might be covered?

Staff

Most staff involvement with copyrighted material will be in photocopying. With the support of the administration, training the clerical staff on copyright of print material will likely be sufficient to raise awareness of what can and can't be copied. Encourage record keeping, especially for multiple copies for classroom use.

Administrators

Getting the attention of the administrator is the key to copyright compliance in a school building. Bringing to his attention materials on copyright settlements in neighboring school districts, and those publicized by copyright compliance groups like AIME and SIIA, can go a long way to opening the eyes of a reluctant administrator. Knowing that the building-level administrator is likely to be named in any copyright infringement action can also get an administrator's attention. As the instructional leader in the school, the building-level administrator is expected to be aware of all educational uses of materials within his purview. Some of the suggestions in the next section, plus those in Chapter 12, will help focus the administrator on the severity of the problem in a given building.

Important Recommendations in Copyright Management

Here are some suggestions to get started in a school that is less than enthusiastic about copyright compliance, where those at risk seem bent on shooting the messenger:

1. Suggest to the principal that you track requests in one area for a grading period. A good place to start is video use. Prepare a report to the administration to let them see the extent of the problem in this area. Remind them that there are many other areas with similar or potentially worse reports. Another option for tracking is to obtain a copy of the free trial program WRQ Express Inventory, SPA Edition from the SIIA and conduct a software audit of up to 100 building computers. Seeing the results in black and white can sometimes generate significant response.

2. Prepare a copyright notification slip that will inform teachers and others that a particular use of material is likely a copyright infringement. Make the wording helpful and informative, not accusatory. Give copies to the principal.

3. Encourage, request, insist on a copyright policy for your building and district. Board-approved policy gives you a firm footing when you are trying to raise the standard of copyright compliance.

4. Educate, educate, educate. Consult with teachers as they plan units, help students document use of others' materials in their work, help administrators consider copyright implications in noncurricular applications. Remember that plagiarism and copyright violation are totally separate and sometimes unrelated issues.

Chapter 12

Implications for Administrators

Whether in charge of a building or district, the school administrator may unexpectedly become embroiled in a legal tangle over the copy machine or the videocassette recorder. Instead of focusing on student performance, she may have to spend hours and days learning abstruse details of copyright law. Even worse, administrators who are unprepared may find themselves and their organizations the subject of expensive litigation, costly even if the school is exonerated.

We are in an era characterized by lawsuit. One lawyer, when asked who should be named in a particularly confusing case, is said to have remarked, "Sue 'em all!" Unfortunately, this is often the mindset in copyright litigation. An administrator who is unaware of, or simply chooses to ignore, copyright violations may suddenly find a cease-and-desist letter on his desk. These letters from attorneys are written in a demanding fashion; violations are spelled out, penalties enumerated, and few options are proposed.

Without the backing of a school board policy or building procedures supporting copyright, an administrator is likely to have little maneuvering room when the ominous letter arrives. Most school district attorneys are better prepared to deal with civil rights charges than with those involving intellectual property. In fact, most details of the day-to-day operation of a building or district are much more pressing than considering the woes of authors and copyright owners. But the fact remains that an administrator who knowingly or unknowingly allows copyright infringement to occur is likely to be named among the defendants in any legal action.

And the district will pay for his carelessness. Penalties can be stiff. Fines begin at $750 per infringement and rise to $30,000. For "innocent infringers" (those who infringe, but had no reason to think they were doing so), fines are not less than $200. If the infringement is considered willful, penalties can be up to $150,000 per violation per day. In the case of computer software infringements, penalties can be as high as $250,000, and the offense may be considered a felony. The administrator need not actually participate in the infringement to be considered responsible, at least in part, for the violation. Some recent court cases may suggest that districts might be found immune to judgment under the 11th Amendment (sovereign immunity), but individual administrators and teachers are not extended this protection.

The truth is that most copyright suits are settled out of court. Only a few well-publicized cases have made the trek through the courts to establish the precedents upon which current practice is based. Even when an infringement action is settled out of court, it still entails much time, considerable stress, and lots of money. Copyright watchdog groups use these settled claims as spoils of war to advertise their victories.

Once the cease-and-desist letter arrives on the administrator's desk, the die is cast. The best plan is to try to minimize losses because, like it or not, the lawyers usually have the goods; the infringements have most likely occurred.

So how can an administrator minimize exposure to copyright litigation? As with most endeavors, plan, plan, plan. The first and most important step is to have a comprehensive copyright policy. If the district has no policy in place, the building chief should establish a building policy. Such a policy should demand adherence to copyright law and establish a system of checks to ensure the law is followed. It also helps if the administration supports the efforts of the librarian and technician in copyright compliance. Tracking and interpreting the many facets of copyright is no mean feat.

Faculties accustomed to free rein in plucking the fruits of authors' and artists' labors will howl that they are being hamstrung. They will moan that they can't conduct their classes without unrestricted access to the many resources they used in the past. They will most likely blame the messenger for the disturbing news.

The building librarian is probably the only person on staff who had some level of copyright training in training for her profession. She attempts to balance the needs of teachers and students while staying within the legal requirements. She should not be thrust alone into the role of "copyright police," however. If building and district policy is to abide by the law, the librarian should not be judge and jury in the procedure.

But the librarian must stand fast, and the administration must provide moral and procedural support. Apologies aren't necessary. As educators, we want to model responsible citizenship to our students. Among the behaviors we endorse is adherence to the laws of the city, state, and country. Copyright is federal law. We would certainly advocate paying income taxes, no matter how much we would wish they were no more. Well, copyright laws may be just as confusing, and we may wish that they allowed as many loopholes as the IRS, but we must still accept them as legal and binding.

Once a policy is in place to require adherence to copyright, someone will need to be available to explain the implications of the law to teachers who may have long ignored it, either from unfamiliarity or intentional oversight. The building librarian is the person most likely to be charged with this task. During their professional training, most librarians have acquired at least a smattering of information about copyright. The library literature is dotted with articles concerning copyright and day-to-day library practice. Also, the library is the source of most of the materials and equipment involved in potential copyright problems. The librarian must have unqualified and open support in monitoring copyright compliance. After all, the object is to keep the entire school community out of trouble. The librarian must not be allowed to become the "bad guy" or the "fall guy" in matters of copyright.

Unequivocal policies supported vigorously by administrators and the school board are essential. It is important that the administrator take a firm stance with staff regarding copyright; expectations should be conveyed to them in no uncertain terms. Educational and informative sessions should be planned to inform the staff annually of their obligations under federal law and district (or building) policy.

Administrators must be ready to counter the "But-we've-always-done-this" argument. They should establish clear procedures for compliance, especially in the areas of photocopying, computer software, and use of audiovisuals. Documentation of compliance is essential, too, so a "paper trail" will exist in case of challenge. Establish a cooperative and collegial atmosphere. Nurture an atmosphere in which one teacher can freely say to another, "I'm not sure that use is within copyright law. Let's get an impartial opinion."

Administrative support for individual creative efforts of staff will encourage them to create, instead of borrow, intellectual property. Additional suggestions from the viewpoint of a building principal may be found in the article "Read my lips: Copyright" by Robin Pennock in the June 1991 issue of *School Library Journal*.

If a building principal or district supervisor is in doubt about the need for administrative involvement and support, a computer software audit may be the one act that demonstrates their value. A software audit will give the administrator a list of every computer program installed on every computer in a district or building. Once equipped with the list, he should ask for documentation of ownership of legal copies of every software program and operating system on the list. Why bother? Because this is exactly what will be required if a representative of a computer software firm should appear at the door with federal marshals bearing a search warrant. A similar exercise could be done with videotapes or filmstrips.

Monitoring compliance is not something the librarian or technician can do alone and without support. Encourage them to bring issues of copyright to the administrative office. Request that teachers document use of video with concrete tie-ins to lesson plans and district curriculum. Don't fall for ruses. Demand hard evidence. Is a showing of *The Lion King* really an appropriate curricular video for a unit on mammals? Encourage alternative rewards other than passive television viewing. Look on the bright side: Copyright compliance can result in better, more creative teaching. Failing to monitor compliance is like leaving the keys in the ignition of a new Corvette with the doors unlocked. Don't be surprised when something unpleasant happens.

Suggestions for Administrators

- *Model copyright compliance*. Request permission before photocopying copyrighted materials for your faculty. (There is limited fair use for copying for staff, anyway.) Mark the copies as "Reprinted with permission from . . . ."

- *Be aware of video use in your building*. How much video is used? Is it all directly related to instruction? Is it appropriate? Teachers never have enough instructional time. Can students afford to spend an hour and a half watching an entertainment video?

- *Request that teachers document each video performance in their lesson plans*. There should be a close correlation between the current lesson, district or state curriculum, and the proposed showing.

- *Insist that teachers clear all video use through your office*. Develop a form that identifies the teacher, the video, and the purpose of the showing. Teachers are less likely to use time-wasting video if they feel the administrator is aware of what is being shown.

- *Know your curriculum*. If the fourth grade studies volcanoes, why is the third grade teacher showing a video on volcanoes?

- *Watch extracurricular activities*. The fair use exemption permits limited use of copyrighted materials in classroom situations. That exemption does not permit free use of copyrighted materials for student council dances, cheerleading posters, or video yearbooks.

- *Look around your building*. What type of decorations do you see? Are they bought from school suppliers, created by teachers, or are they copied from greeting cards, cartoons, movie characters, and the like?

- *Enlist the assistance of those staff members most likely to be aware of copyright violations in the building*. Teacher aides know what types of materials are being photocopied. Librarians know what video is being shown and what multimedia is being appropriated. Technicians know what software is installed. They can assist you with record keeping, but they shouldn't be put into the role of copyright police.

- *Help teachers find creative, nonvideo ways to reward students*. Reward videos are public performances and require payment of royalties or written exemption from the copyright holder.

- *Keep accurate purchase records for audiovisual materials and computer software*. These records should be retained as long as the materials are in use. The records may be needed if there should ever be a question of legality.

- ***Purchase a performance license for your building*** to show some noninstructional videos for rewards or as quick fill-ins when events get rained out or teachers are tied up in conferences. Don't let it become a babysitter.

- ***Assist staff in their efforts to stay copyright-compliant***. Make sure there are enough copies of computer software (or appropriate licenses) to cover each machine that will use the software. Budget for record keeping supplies, compliance reminder stickers for equipment, and sufficient consumables.

- ***Keep an upbeat attitude***. Long-held habits die hard. Encourage efforts to stay compliant. Commiserate with those who complain that their favorite activities are no longer permitted. Look on the bright side: You'll see how creative your teachers can be.

- ***Remember that a good faith effort and an honest accounting can go a long way*** when someone does slip up. Everyone makes occasional mistakes. Learn from them and go on.

Chapter *13*

The Importance of a Copyright Policy

Why bother to have a copyright policy? A devil's advocate would say that there is no need for a policy. Why state the obvious? There is no policy requiring compliance with the local building code, is there? It's just common sense. One complies with the building code because it is the law. Doesn't one also comply with copyright because it is the law? Everyone obeys copyright; there's no need for a policy. Besides, who's going to catch a violator?

Well, the devil's advocate is oversimplifying. Do police departments expect all motorists to observe the speed limit because it is the law? Hardly. That's why they purchase and use radar units. Publishers and media producers are of a similar opinion. They know people will attempt to violate their rights under copyright, and they exercise various means to discover and prosecute the offenders. And while an occasional inadvertent slip might be overlooked, widespread or systematic infringement is likely to bring a hailstorm of litigation.

The purpose of a copyright policy is to state the institution's intention to abide by the law. AIME (Association for Information Media and Equipment), the copyright watchdog group, boasts of its successes in redressing copyright infringement. While most of the cases are settled out of court, AIME publishes many of the settlements in its periodic newsletters. The majority of the settlements involve the establishment of an institutional policy regarding copyright as well as comprehensive training and plans for tracking and monitoring copyright compliance. Agreements to discharge key employees or place official letters of reprimand in personnel files are sometimes included in these out-of-court settlements.

Having an institutional copyright compliance policy is one way to beat the producers to the punch. AIME makes a good case with the following statement:

"AIME takes the position that a copyright policy is important for an educational entity to develop. It helps to avoid confusion on the part of the staff and administrators and takes a definitive position on the importance of knowing the law and obeying it. A copyright policy also has the potential to insulate the agency or institution and administrators from liability if an infringement action were to be instituted because of activities by individuals contrary to the policy and against the law" (Dohra, n.d.).

AIME produces a packet of information on developing an institutional copyright policy. Included in the packet is a small booklet titled *A viewer's guide to copyright law: What every school, college and public library should know*. The primary author of this booklet is Ivan Bender, an attorney specializing in copyright issues. The booklet has an excellent section on development of copyright policy.

Appendix E is an example of a district-wide copyright policy adopted in 1993. Several points in the policy are worth noting:

- The policy states the institution's intention to abide by the letter and spirit of the copyright law and the associated congressional guidelines.

- The policy covers all types of materials including print, nonprint, graphics, and computer software.

- The liability for noncompliance with copyright rests with the individual using the work.

- Training is mandated for all personnel who might have need to make copies.

- The person using the materials must be able to produce, on request, copyright justification for its use.

Some authorities recommend that additional measures be included in a policy, such as the assignment of a copyright officer, requiring the district to develop a copyright manual for all employees, requiring notices to be affixed to all copy-capable equipment, and even reprinting the entire law and guidelines (Vleck, p. 10; AIME, p. 7).

Regardless of the wording of the policy, simply having a policy that states institutional intent to obey the law will provide some small measure of protection. However, the more the faculty and staff know about copyright and the management of copyrighted materials, the better protected the organization and the employees are from threat of suit. If an infringement were to occur, the administration that has undertaken a thorough copyright education program could present a credible case that they did not condone the activity and that they had taken vigorous action to prevent infringement. The infringing employee, though, would have a poor chance of claiming "innocent infringement," a defense for those who claim they had no knowledge they were infringing, because the institution would have records of staff development in correct application of copyright principles.

A further measure to protect the institution from individual acts of infringement is to have employees sign a statement indicating they have been informed of copyright laws and guidelines and that they will abide by both the institutional policy and the applicable laws. (See Appendix A.) This is similar to the OSHA requirement that employees be informed of hazards of chemicals in the work place. Frequently employees are required to view a training tape or attend a staff development session on a topic for which they are "signed off." Such record-keeping indemnifies the organization from claims of negligence in informing the employees of potential hazards. Copyright infringement is certainly hazardous for both the individual employee and the organization, and having employees sign a compliance agreement or sign in at a staff development session on copyright at the beginning of the school year is not an unbearable burden when tracked at the building level.

The most efficient way to develop a copyright policy is to search out examples of model policies. AIME provides multiple examples of acceptable policies in its copyright policy development kit. A custom-developed copyright policy can be quickly assembled by cutting and pasting the best parts of the samples. Administrators, librarians, and television and media people should all have a say in the final wording. Bringing in an outside expert may be the best way to persuade doubters who believe a comprehensive policy isn't necessary.

The final draft of the policy should go to the district's legal counsel for approval, because collective bargaining agreements and teacher contracts may affect wording of policies. A spokesperson should be prepared to appear before the board to underscore the importance of the policy and explain the risk of leaving copyright compliance to individual employees. And a plan should be in place to train employees and monitor compliance in libraries, classrooms, and offices.

Copyright Compliance Agreement

Middletown Independent School District
Copyright Compliance Agreement

I have been informed of the appropriate uses of instructional media, fair use guidelines, and the copyright compliance policy of the Middletown Independent School District. I, the undersigned, acknowledge that I understand these policies and guidelines and that any uses I may make of instructional materials or audio-visual equipment in a classroom setting will be in accordance with both federal law and said policies and guidelines.

_____

Teacher

_____

Date

_____

Campus

Appendix B

Copyright Do's and Don'ts for School Librarians

DO make sure that all audiovisual material shown to students is directly related to the curriculum. Be especially aware of film ratings (G, PG, R).

DO ask your faculty to sign a copyright compliance agreement.

DO write the record date on all videos you tape.

DO write the required erase date on all videos you tape. This date will vary with the program. See advertisement of program, flyer from producer, or calculate fair use date.

DO keep receipts and purchase orders for all videos and computer software. Keep the catalog (or pertinent pages) to verify purchase of public performance rights.

DO require teachers to verify taping date and source for all home-taped videos. Fair use guidelines say that tapes must be used for classroom instruction within 10 days of taping. After that date, the tape may only be used for evaluation for possible purchase. Erase after 45 days.

DO write for permission to retain tapes of useful programs. The worst a copyright holder can do is say no.

DO post a copyright notice similar to that on your photocopy machine on VCRs, overhead projectors, opaque projectors, computers, and cassette recorders.

DON'T create anthologies on tape or the photocopier. Copying an article, poem, or excerpt is fine, but combining them into a "new work" is not permitted.

DON'T apologize for obeying federal law. If you would like a free copy of the law, write to the Library of Congress and request Circular 92.

DON'T show films or videos for reinforcement or reward. Encourage teachers to try popcorn and soft drink parties, stickers, or free time. You may rent movies for such performances, paying a minimal public performance fee, from suppliers such as Kit Parker Films. *Video rental stores cannot authorize you to give public performances.*

DON'T lend VCRs with patch cords. Watch for questionable situations. For instance, why would a teacher need two VCRs except to copy tapes?

DON'T copy commercial computer software, except to make an archival copy (one that isn't used).

DON'T copy cartoon or TV or film characters for decorations, bulletin boards, or handouts. Purchasing clip art, duplicator books, and bulletin board figures is acceptable, but you may not enlarge, modify, or change the medium (e.g., make slides or coloring sheets).

DO remember that the person who pushes the button is also liable. So is the principal if she knows copyright is being violated. We recommend you notify in writing both the principal and teacher when you are aware of copyright infringement. Keep a copy in your own file.

DO keep a copy of Kidsnet or Cable in the Classroom to verify taping rights from the various networks. Kidsnet also lists supporting materials and addresses where inexpensive copies of non-tapeable programs can be obtained.

DO encourage teachers to use fast forward. Often only a portion of a video will make as effective a point as an entire film. Also, some producers will allow use of "excerpts" when they will not allow use of an entire program. Write for permission.

DON'T tape programs off cable without investigating the tape rights first. Only programs taped off the air (VHF and UHF channels) can be taped without express permission. Look for this permission in teachers' guides that the various networks and program producers send out. These guides will also tell you the retention rights (e.g., seven days plus fair use, one year, life of tape). Keep a photocopy of the permission with the tape at all times, and make sure there is a copyright notice on each tape.

DON'T tape a program because you know a teacher will ask for it later. Requests to tape programs must come from a teacher in advance and in writing. Also, requests to tape programs must come from the "bottom up," i.e., your teachers can ask you to tape programs, but your principal may not.

Useful Sources of Information

AIME (Association for Information Media and Equipment)
P.O. Box 1173
Clarksdale, MS 38614
601-624-9355
<www.aime.org>

American Society of Composers, Authors & Publishers (ASCAP)
One Lincoln Plaza
New York, NY 10023
212-621-6000
e-mail: *info@ascap.com*
<www.ascap.com>

Association of American Publishers
71 Fifth Avenue
New York, NY 10003
212-255-0200

Audio-Cine Films, Inc.
8462, Sherbrooke St. E.
Montreal, PQ, H2L 1B2
Canada
800-289-8887
<http://www.acf-film.com/>

Bell & Howell Information and Learning
300 N. Zeeb Road
P.O. Box 1346
Ann Arbor, MI 48016-1345
800-521-0600
<www.umi.com>
e-mail: *info@umi.com*

Broadcast Music, Inc. (BMI)
320 W. 57th Street
New York, NY 10019
212-586-2000

Business Software Alliance
1150 18th Street, N.W. Suite 700
Washington, D.C. 20036
202-872-5500
<www.bsa.org>

Cable in the Classroom Magazine
1800 N. Beauregard Street, Suite 100
Alexandria, VA 22311
800-743-5355
www.ciconline.com/>

Canadian Musical Reproduction Rights Agency Ltd.
56 Wellesley St. W. #320
Toronto, Ont.
Canada M5S 2S3
(416) 926-1966
<http://www.cmrra.ca/home4/home4.html>

Cancopy
1 Yonge Street, Suite 1900
Toronto, ON
M5E 1E5
800-893-5777
<www.cancopy.com/>

Christian Copyright Licensing, Inc.
17201 NE Sacramento Street
Portland, OR 97230
(800) 234-2446
<http://www.ccli.com/>

Church Music Publishers Association
PO Box 158992
Nashville, TN 37215
615-791-0273
<http://www.cmpamusic.org/>

Copyright Clearance Center
222 Rosewood Drive
Danvers, MA 01923
978-750-8400
<www.copyright.com>

Discovery Channel School
P.O. Box 970
Oxon Hill, MD 20750-0970
800-321-1832
<school.discovery.com>

Films for the Humanities & Sciences

(source of copyright-cleared sound effects)
PO Box 2053
Princeton, NJ
800-257-5126
<www.films.com>

FTC Publishing Group

(source of multimedia sound files)
P.O. Box 1361
Bloomington, IL 61702-1361
888-237-6740
<www.ftcpublishing.com>

Harry Fox Agency

711 Third Avenue
New York, NY 10017
212-370-5330

Kidsnet

6856 Eastern Avenue N.W., Suite 208
Washington, DC 20012
202-291-1400
202-882-7315 FAX
<www.kidsnet.org>

Kit Parker Films

(rental for public performance)
P.O. Box 16022
Monterey, CA 93942-6022
800-538-5838
<www.kitparker.com>

Motion Picture Association of America

15503 Ventura Blvd.
Encino, CA 91436
818-995-6600

Motion Picture Licensing Corporation

5455 Centinela Avenue
Los Angeles, CA 90066-6970
800-462-8855

Movie Licensing USA

201 S. Jefferson Ave.
Saint Louis, MO 63103-9954
877-321-1300
<www.movlic.com/>

Music Publishers Association of the U.S.

PMB 246
1562 First Avenue
New York, NY 10028
<www.mpa.org/>

National Music Publishers Association

711 Third Avenue
New York, NY 10017
212-370-5330
<www.nmpa.org>

National Writer's Union

National Office East
113 University Place 6th Fl.
New York, NY 10003
212-254-0279
Fax:(212) 254-0673
<www.nwu.org/>

Public Domain Report

P.O. Box 3102
Margate, NJ 08402
800-827-9401
<www.pubdomain.com>

Publisher's Toolbox

2310 Darwin Road
Madison, WI 53704
800-390-0461
<www.pubtool.com>

Software and Information Industry Association

1730 M Street, N.W.
Washington, DC 20036
202-452-1600
<www.siia.net>
This group also provides a software inventory management package
in either PC or Macintosh format.

Soundzabound Music Library

P.O. Box 492199
Atlanta, GA 30349-2199
888-834-1792
<www.soundzabound.com>

Swank Motion Pictures, Inc.

(rental for public performance)
350 Vanderbilt Motor Parkway, Suite 203
Hauppauge, New York 11787-4305
800-876-5577

United States Copyright Office

Library of Congress
Washington, DC 20559
202-479-0700
202-707-9100 (to order forms and circulars)
Main Web site <lcweb.loc.gov/copyright/>
Circular 1, Copyright Basics <lcweb.loc.gov/copyright/circs/circ1.html>
Copyright law, complete text <lcweb.loc.gov/copyright/title17/>
Copyright registration requirements <www.loc.gov/copyright/reg.html>

Appendix D

Copyright Warning Notices

All interlibrary loan request forms must include the following notice (Code of Federal Regulations, Title 37, Section 201.14). It must be printed within a prominent box on the actual order form. The notice may be on the front of the form, or adjacent to the section requiring the patron's signature. The notice cannot be in type any smaller than that used throughout the form, and in no case may it be smaller than 8-point type. The notice must be clearly apparent, legible, and comprehensible to even a casual viewer of the form. Standard ALA ILL forms available from library supply houses comply with this requirement.

The same notice must be displayed at the place where ILL orders are taken. Such notice must be printed on heavy paper, in type no less than 18 points in size. It must be placed so as to be clearly visible, legible, and comprehensible near the place where ILL orders are accepted. This notice is also appropriate for any location or form where library copy orders are taken.

NOTICE

WARNING CONCERNING COPYRIGHT RESTRICTIONS

The copyright law of the United States (Title 17, United States Code) governs the making of photocopies or other reproductions of copyrighted material.

Under certain conditions specified in the law, libraries and archives are authorized to furnish a photocopy or other reproduction. One of these specified conditions is that the photocopy or reproduction is not to be "used for any purpose other than private study, scholarship, or research." If a user makes a request for, or later uses, a photocopy or reproduction for purposes in excess of "fair use," that user may be liable for copyright infringement.

This institution reserves the right to refuse to accept a copying order if, in its judgment, fulfillment of the order would involve violation of the copyright law.

Photocopies made by libraries, both for interlibrary loan and for patrons, should be marked with the original copyright notice. If an item has no copyright notice, a notice of possible copyright restrictions must be added. While specific wording isn't detailed in the law, many libraries use wording similar to the following:

Notice: This material may be protected by Copyright Law (Title 17 U.S. Code).

Appendix E

Sample Copyright Policy

It is the intent of the Mesquite Independent School District, its board of trustees, staff, and students, to adhere to the provisions of current copyright laws and congressional guidelines. Employees and students are to adhere to all provisions of Title 17 of the United States Code, titled "Copyrights," and other relative federal legislation and guidelines related to the duplication, retention, and use of copyrighted materials.

Specifically:

- Unlawful copies of copyrighted materials may not be produced on district-owned equipment.

- Unlawful copies of copyrighted material may not be used with district-owned equipment, within district-owned facilities, or at district-sponsored functions.

- The legal and insurance protection of the district will not be extended to employees who unlawfully copy and use copyrighted materials.

- Employees who make or use copies of copyrighted materials in their jobs are expected to be familiar with published provisions regarding fair use and public display, and are further expected to be able to provide their supervisor, upon request, the justification under sections 107 or 110 of USC 17 for materials that have been used or copied.

- Employees who use copyrighted materials that do not fall within fair use or public display guidelines will be able to substantiate that the materials meet one of the following tests:

  - The materials have been purchased from an authorized vendor by the individual or the district and a record of the purchase exists.

  - The materials are copies covered by a licensing agreement between the copyright owner and the district or the individual employee.

  - The materials are being previewed or demonstrated by the user to reach a decision about future purchase or licensing and a valid agreement exists that allows for such use.

Reprinted courtesy of Mesquite (TX) Independent School District.

Appendix F

Release Form

Middletown School District Publication Release Form

I, the undersigned, having full authority to execute this Release on behalf of myself and on behalf of _____ _____(child's name) of _____ (school name) hereby grant permission to MIDDLETOWN SCHOOL DISTRICT (hereinafter called "MSD") to use the following materials provided by me or on my child's behalf to MSD, for the purposes identified below:

My or my child's: (initial where appropriate) _____ Name _____ Voice _____Likeness _____ Quotes _____ Papers, articles, poems or other written material as specified:

_____

_____

Graphics, photographs, or other artwork as specified:

_____

_____

I warrant and represent that the materials submitted under this agreement are owned by and/or are original to me or my child, and/or I have full authority from the owner of said materials to permit MSD to use said materials in the manner described below: _____ Newspapers, magazines, other print publications _____ Television or radio _____ Internet or computer network _____ Presentation for teaching, staff development or professional conference _____ Public display or performance.

I understand that MSD is and shall be the exclusive owner of any and all right, title, and interest, including copyright, to any and all materials into which the aforementioned items are incorporated, except as to my preexisting rights in any of the items herein released.

Date: _____

Signature: _____

Name/Relationship: _____

Address: _____

_____

Telephone: _____

Appendix G

Copyright and Plagiarism Guidelines for Students

1. You may make a single photocopy of any material you need to do your schoolwork, or for your own personal research. You may keep the copies you make as long as you like, but you may not sell them, nor may you make copies of your copies.

2. You must respect the copyright of the materials you use. Only the creators or the persons or companies who own the copyright may make copies of the material, except as noted above. You may not modify or change the material, nor may you perform or display the material except in conjunction with class work.

3. You may use copyrighted material to do your schoolwork, but if you use an author's ideas you must give the author credit, either in the text or in a footnote. If you use an author's words, you must put the words in quotation marks or other indication of direct quotation. Failure to give credit to the author is plagiarism. If you use an extensive amount of a single work, you must obtain permission.

4. Use of copyrighted materials outside of regular class work requires written permission of the copyright holder. This includes graphic material such as cartoon characters on posters or other spirit or decorative matter.

5. You may not copy computer software from the school computers.

6. Information received from the school computers may be used only for regular schoolwork or personal research.

7. The source of any information used in your schoolwork should be acknowledged in the format prescribed by the teacher. Use of another's intellectual work without attribution is plagiarism, as outlined in the Student Code of Conduct.

Significant Copyright Law Section References

(All references are to U. S. Code Title 17.)

Moral rights: Section 106-106(a).
Fair use: Section 107
Library copying: Section 108
First sale doctrine: Section 109(a)
Circulation of computer software: Section 109(b.1.A ff)
Public display of lawful copies: Section 109(c)
Face-to-face teaching exceptions: Section 110(1)
Distance learning performances: Section 110(2)
Digital audio performances: Section 114(d) – (j)
Computer software requirements: Section 117
Architectural works: Section 120
Special exceptions for the blind and physically disabled: Section 121
Duration of copyright: Section 302
Certain exemptions for librarians and educators: Section 504 (c)
No electronic theft: Section 506
OSP liability: Section 512
Technological protections: Section 1201-1205

Bibliography of Works Cited and Selected Works on Copyright

American Library Association. *Model policy concerning college and university photocopying for classroom research and library reserve use.* Chicago: ALA, 1982.

_____. *Video and copyright.* [online] www.ala.org/library/fact7.html

Association for Information Media and Equipment. Press release. Elkader, IA: AIME. 1990.

_____. *A viewer's guide to copyright law: What every school, college, and public library should know.* Elkader, IA: AIME. 1987.

Barlow, John Perry. "The economy of ideas" [online] www.wired.com/wired/archive/2.03/economy.ideas.html

Bender, Ivan. "What copyright laws tell us," *Media & Methods.* March/April, 1992.

_____. "The Internet—It's not free and never was," *AIME News.* Summer, 1996.

Berman, D. "Re: Questionable videotapes." Discussion on liability in the use of copyrighted videotapes. CNI-COPYRIGHT. (May 13, 1993).

Bielefield Arlene and Lawrence Cheeseman. *Interpreting and negotiating licensing agreements: A guidebook for the library, research, and teaching professions.* New York: Neal-Schuman, 1999.

_____. *Technology and Copyright Law: A Guidebook for the Library, Research and Teaching Professions.* New York: Neal-Schuman, 1997.

Copyright Information Services. *Official fair-use guidelines: Complete texts of four official documents arranged for use by educators.* 4th ed. Friday Harbor, WA, 1985, 1987.

Copyright Office. Circular R21: Reproduction of copyrighted works by educators and librarians. Washington, D.C.: Library of Congress, 1992.

Crews. Indiana University Online Copyright Tutorial, Bloomington, IN, 1998.

Dohra, Allen. Copyright information packet. Elkader, IA, AIME, (n.d.).

Dukelow, Ruth H. *The library copyright guide.* Washington, D.C.: Copyright Information Services, Association for Educational Communications & Technology, 1992.

Education Software Management. *A K-12 Guide to Legal Software Use*. Software and Information Industry Association, 1994.

Ensign, David James. "Fax—a special case," *The Bookmark*. Winter, 1992.

Fishman, Steven. *The copyright handbook*. 5th ed. Berkeley, CA, Nolo, 2000.

Goldstein, Paul. *Copyright*. 2nd ed. 4 vols. New York: Aspen Law & Business, 1998.

Hoart, Helen. "Re: Copyright infringement." Letter to Report on Education Research subscribers. c. 1992.

Jackson, Mary E. "Library to library," *Wilson Library Bulletin*. December, 1991.

Jassin, Lloyd J. and Steven C. Schechter, *The copyright permission and libel handbook*. New York, John Wiley, 1998.

Jensen, Mary Brandt. "I'm not my brother's keeper: Why libraries shouldn't worry too much about what patrons do with library materials at home," *The Bookmark*. Winter, 1992.

Kruppenbacher, Frank. "Re: CC and copyright." Discussion on the addition of closed captioning to commercial videotapes. CNI-COPYRIGHT, June 14, 1993.

Marshall, Patrick G. "Software piracy," *CQ Researcher*. May 21, 1993.

National School Boards Association. *Legal Issues & Education Technology: A School Leader's Guide*. Alexandria, VA, 1999.

Nimmer, Melville B. and David. *Nimmer on Copyright*. 10 vols. New York: Matthew Bender & Co., 1999.

Reed, Mary Hutchings. *Videotapes: copyright and licensing considerations for schools and libraries*. Syracuse, NY: ERIC Clearinghouse on Information Resources. (ERIC Document Reproduction Service No. ED 308 855), June, 1989.

Schneider, Bruce. "Practice safe multimedia: wear a copyright." Newsmedia. December 1992.

Shepherd, Carol Ruth. "Re: Sales of videotapes." Discussion on permissions required for sale of videotapes of school performances. CNI-COPYRIGHT, May 24, 1996.

Sinofsky, Esther. "Re: Closed-caption videotape conversion." Discussion on the addition   of closed captioning to commercial videotapes. CNI-COPYRIGHT, June 14, 1993.

Sivin, J. P. and E. R. Bialo. *Ethical use of information technologies in education: important issues for America's schools*. Washington, D.C. : U.S. Department of Justice, 1992.

Software and Information Industry Association. *Software Management Guide*. 1994.

Stanek, D. J. "Videotapes, computer programs, and the library," *Information technology and libraries*. March 1986.

Stim, Richard. *Getting permission: How to license & clear copyrighted materials online & off*. Berkeley, CA, Nolo Press, 2000.

Talab, R. S. *Commonsense copyright: a guide for educators and librarians*. Jefferson, N.C., McFarland & Co., 1999.

Texas Education Agency. *Copyright: school and "fair use."* Austin: TEA, 1984.

Vleck, Charles W. *Copyright policy development: a resource book for educators*. Friday Harbor, WA : Copyright Information Services, 1987.

Appendix J

Important Internet Links for Copyright Information

Agreement on Guidelines for Classroom Copying in Not-For-Profit Educational Institutions with Respect to Books and Periodicals
<www.musiclibraryassoc.org/Copyright/guidebks.htm>

American Library Association Copyright and Intellectual Property
<www.ala.org/work/copyright.html>

Association for Instructional Media and Equipment
<www.aime.org/>

Brad Templeton's "Ten Big Myths about Copyright"
<www.templetons.com/brad/copymyths.html>

Canadian Intellectual Property Office
<http://strategis.ic.gc.ca/sc_mrksv/cipo/welcome/welcom-e.html>

Complying with the Digital Millennium Copyright Act
<www.utsystem.edu/OGC/IntellectualProperty/dmcaisp.htm>

Copying under copyright: a practical guide (music copying)
<http://host.mpa.org/copyrigh.html>

Copyright for educators.
<falcon.jmu.edu/~ramseyil/copy.htm>

Copyright guidelines, Jefferson County Public Schools, CO.
<http://204.98.1.2/plmc/copyright.html>

Copyright Implementation Manual, Groton, CT, Public Schools
<www.groton.k12.ct.us/mts/cimhp01.htm>

Copyright Notices for Supervised Library Copying:
Updated Information for Library Services
<www.iupui.edu/~copyinfo/copying.html>

Copyright Office Designation by Service Provider of Agent
for Notification of Claims for Copyright Infringement
<http://lcweb.loc.gov/copyright/onlinesp/>

Copyright permission pages
<www.law.wfu.edu/library/copyright/>

Copyright timeline
<arl.cni.org/info/frn/copy/timeline.html>

Copyright Web site
<www.benedict.com>

Copyright workshop
<www.cyberbee.com/copyrt.html>

Distance Learning Guidelines report of the Register of Copyright
<lcweb.loc.gov/copyright/disted>

Fair Use Guidelines For Educational Multimedia
<www.utsystem.edu/ogc/intellectualproperty/ccmcguid.htm>

Friends of Active Copyright Education
<http://law.duke.edu/copyright/face/index.htm>

Guidelines for Educational Uses of Music
<www.musiclibraryassoc.org/Copyright/guidemus.htm>

Guidelines for Off-Air Recordings of Broadcast Programming
for Educational Purposes
<www.musiclibraryassoc.org/Copyright/guiderec.htm>

Library and Classroom Use of Copyrighted Videotapes and Computer Software
<www.ifla.org/documents/infopol/copyright/ala-1.txt>

MARC record guidelines for copyright management information
<lcweb.loc.gov/marc/bibliographic/ecbdnot2.html#mrcb540>

PBS Teacher Source
<www.pbs.org/teachersource/copyright/copyright.shtm>

PDInfo – Public domain music
<www.pdinfo.com/>

Public Domain Report
<pubdomain.com>

Sample off-air videotape label
<www.pbs.org/teachersource/copyright/copyright_sample_label.shtm>

Software and Information Industry Association. Software Use & the Law
<www.siia.net/piracy/copyright/law.asp>

Stanford University. Copyright and Fair Use Web site
<fairuse.stanford.edu/>

SupportNet Online – Copyright and fair use
<supportnet.merit.edu/Webclubs/copyright.html>

Tell it to the judge (copyright quiz)
<www.news.com/Quiz/Entry/0%2C63%2C%2C00.html>

University of Texas System Crash Course on Copyright
<www.utsystem.edu/ogc/intellectualproperty/cprtindx.htm>

Use of Music on a Multimedia Web site
<www.ivanhoffman.com/music.html>

Using Software: A Guide to the Ethical and Legal Use
of Software for Members of the Academic Community
<www.ifla.org/documents/infopol/copyright/educom.txt>

Video Public Performance Rights
<www.willamette.edu/news/bbn/jan00/video.html>

A visit to Copyright Bay
<www.nmjc.cc.nm.us/copyrightbay/>

World Book and Copyright Day – UNESCO
<www.unesco.org/general/eng/events/book/book.html>

Sources of Audiovisual Works with Public Performance Rights

NOTE: Not all media sold by these producers and distributors may have public performance rights, but all listed companies sell some materials with public performance rights. Some sell the same materials with and without such rights. Order carefully and compare prices. Also note that rights may apply only to items purchased directly from the producer, not through jobbers. An updated version of this list may be found at:

<courses.unt.edu/csimpson/cright/ppr.htm>

Annenberg/CPB
401 9th Street, NW
Washington, DC 20004
800-LEARNER
<www.learner.org/>

Bullfrog Films (all titles except "home video versions")
P.O. Box 149
Oley, PA 19547
610-779-8226
<www.bullfrogfilms.com>

California Newsreel
149 Ninth Street
San Francisco, CA 94103
415-621-6196
<www.newsreel.org>

Cambridge Documentary Films, Inc.
P.O. Box 390385
Cambridge, MA 02139-0004
617-484-3993
<www1.shore.net/~cdf/>

Chip Taylor Communications (discount, no-rights versions available)
2 East View Drive
Derry, NH 03038
800-876-CHIP (2447)
<www.chiptaylor.com/index.htm>

The Cinema Guild
1697 Broadway, Suite 506
New York, NY 10019
212-246-5522
<www.cinemaguild.com/home.html>

Classroom Video
4739 University Way, NE, Suite 1606
Seattle, WA 98105
800-665-4121
<www.classroomvideo.com>

CLEARVUE/eav
6465 North Avondale Avenue
Chicago, Illinois. 60631-1996
800-253-2788
<www.clearvue.com/index.html>

Disney Educational Productions (see Web site for specific limitations)
105 Terry Drive
Newtown, PA 18940
800-295-5010
<disney.go.com/educational/teacherstore/index.html>

Educational Video Network, Inc.
1401 19th St.
Huntsville, TX 77340
800-762-0060
<www.edvidnet.com/>

Fanlight Productions
4196 Washington St, Suite 2
Boston, MA 02131
800-937-4113
<www.fanlight.com/>

Films for the Humanities and Sciences
PO Box 2053
Princeton, NJ
800-257-5126
<www.films.com>

GPN (Reading Rainbow and others)
P.O. Box 80669
Lincoln, NE 68501-0669
800-228-4630
<gpn.unl.edu/index.html>
* Note: only for titles bought directly from the producer. Reading Rainbow titles
bought from jobbers do not include public performance rights.

Insight Media (limited titles)
2162 Broadway
New York, NY 10024-0621
800-233-9910
<www.insight-media.com/win.html>

Instructional Video (all except those marked HUO "home use only")
2219 C Street
Lincoln, NE 68502
800.228.0164

International Historic Films, Inc. (most titles)
P.O. Box 29035
Chicago, IL 60629 USA
773-927-2900
<ihffilm.com/info.html>

Library Video Company (Schlessinger Media video titles only)
7 E. Wynnewood Road
Wynnewood, PA 19096
800-843-3620
<www.libraryvideo.com>

Lucerne Media
37 Ground Pine Road
Morris Plains, NJ 07950
800-341-2293
<www.lucernemedia.com>

Media for the Arts (limited titles)
360 Thames Street, Suite 2N
Newport, Rhode Island 02840
800-554-6008

USANoodlehead Network
107 Intervale Ave.
 Burlington, VT 05401
800-639-5680

PBS Video (all lines except PBS Home Video)
PO Box 751089
Charlotte, NC 28275
877-PBS-SHOP

Phoenix Learning Group (including Phoenix, BFA and Coronet)
(most products)
2349 Chaffee Drive
St. Louis, MO 63146
800-221-1274

Princeton Book Company
P.O. Box 831
Hightstown, New Jersey 08520-0831

Pyramid Media, Inc.
P.O.Box 1048
Santa Monica, CA 90406
800-421-2304
<www.pyramidmedia.com>

Questar, Inc.
680 N. Lake Shore Dr., Suite 900
Chicago, IL 60611
312-397-2156
<www.questar1.com>

Revels, Inc. (videos only)
Department R
80 Mount Auburn Street
Watertown, Massachusetts 02472-3930
617-972-8300
<www.revels.org/langstaff_video.html>

Rich-Heape Films, Inc. (limited titles)
5952 Royal Lane, Suite 254-4,
Dallas, Texas 75230
888-600-2922

Scholastic, Inc. (all titles except those marked "Home Use Only")
555 Broadway
New York, NY 10012-3999
<www.scholastic.com>
800-724-6527

Sunburst Communications
101 Castleton Street
Pleasantville, NY 10570
914-747-3310

SVE & Churchill Media
6677 North Northwest Highway
Chicago, IL 60631
800-829-1900
<www.svemedia.com>

The Video Project
200 Estates Dr.
Ben Lomond, CA 95005
800-4-PLANET
<www.videoproject.org>

Weston Woods (all titles except those marked "Home use only")
265 Post Road West
Westport, CT 06880
800-243-5020

Appendix L   **Copyright Brochure**

The following brochure is designed to be reproduced at 115% onto 2 sides of standard 81/2" x 11" paper and tri-folded. Reproduction for a single school building is permitted as long as copyright management information remains intact. For reproduction beyond a single building, please contact Linworth Publishing for fees.

Audiovisual

How can I use a radio or television program in class?

You may record a program as it is broadcast by a local radio or television station; you may, within 10 school days of recording the program, use it once with each class for instructional purposes and once again for reinforcement. From the 11th day through the 45th calendar day after the broadcast, it may be used only for evaluation purposes; after that period, you must erase the recording unless you have obtained permission (from the copyright holder) to keep it.

You may make copies of the recording to meet the needs of other teachers, but all copies share the same time restrictions as the original. Unless you have specific permission (as with National Geographic specials and some Project Discovery programs), you may not use recordings made from cable-only television channels. See *Cable in the Classroom* magazine for permissions.

I have a 16mm film; it would be easier to use on video. Can I have it copied?

To make a copy of an audiovisual work other than one recorded under the off-air taping guidelines (above) requires permission of the copyright holder. In most cases, a polite, well-written letter explaining the circumstances will result in permission being granted, but don't make the copy until you receive permission.

We have a video program that was very expensive to purchase and I'm worried that it might be damaged by accident. Since it's okay to make a backup of computer software, isn't it okay to make a backup copy of this tape?

No. In order to make a backup copy of a video program, you must have purchased "archival rights" from the copyright holder or receive written permission prior to making the copy.

May I show rented tapes in class?

Yes, if you rent a tape that applies to your instructional needs and use it in "face-to-face" instruction, and if the showing occurs in a classroom or other instructional place, and if only teachers and students in the class view the showing. In such a situation, the showing would fall under the fair use guidelines.

No, if the tape is to be shown as a "reward." Rental stores do not ordinarily purchase the public performance rights required for a reward or entertainment showing to a public group (a class constitutes a public group and therefore doesn't qualify for a fair use exemption.) Many libraries purchase public performance rights, but you should ask.

I wish to remove an objectionable scene from a movie I plan to show. May I edit the scene out?

You aren't required to show an entire video, but you may not edit the program. If you wish to skip the objectionable scene, you can fast-forward past it.

Administrative note:

Always use discretion in showing rented videos in your classroom, making certain that you choose only those that are appropriate. Check the ratings regarding language, sex, violence, nudity, and morality, and if in doubt, don't show it.

This brochure was reprinted from Copyright for Schools: A Practical Guide, 3rd edition, by Carol Simpson, Linworth Publishing, ©2001.

---

cop•y•right \‑, rīt \ n (1735): The exclusive right to reproduce, publish, and sell the matter and form of a literary, musical, or artistic work.

Print

What can I copy?

You may make a single copy of a chapter from a book; a newspaper or magazine article; a short story, short essay, or short poem; or a single chart, graph, diagram, drawing, cartoon, or picture from a book, periodical, or newspaper for personal, research, or classroom use.

May I make multiple copies for classroom use?

Yes, but copy length is limited: You may copy a whole poem only if it is under 250 words (or a 250-word excerpt from a longer poem); a whole article, story, or essay only if it is less than 2,500 words (or an excerpt if it is less than 1,000 words or 10 percent of a work, whichever is less); a single chart, graph, diagram, drawing, cartoon, or picture per book or magazine; and only two pages of a picture book (as long as the two pages don't contain more than 10 percent of the total text of the book).

How many copies may I make?

You may make a single copy of the items listed above if the copy is for personal use, research or teaching. For multiple copies for classroom use you can make only enough copies for each pupil enrolled in the course, i.e., no "extra" copies. You may not copy more than one entire item (or two excerpts) from a single author, or three articles from a single book or periodical volume during one class term (semester or year, depending on the course). You cannot have more than nine instances of multiple copying per course during a class term.

When and how may I use the copies?

You, the teacher, must make the decision to make the copies. (Your principal or supervisor is not allowed to tell you to make copies of copyrighted material.) You must decide to make the copies so close to the time you would need them in class that writing for and receiving permission would be impractical. (Two weeks would be a reasonable time.) You may copy the item for only one course (all your English I classes, for example.) Each item copied must have a notice of copyright.

This sounds hard! Why don't you just tell me what I can't copy?

You may never copy, in any form, items intended to be consumable. That includes workbook pages, standardized tests, coloring books, answer sheets, and test booklets. You also may not make so many different copies that you are, in effect, creating your own textbook. Copying cannot take the place of books, publisher's reprints, or magazine subscriptions. You can't charge students for copying above the actual cost of the copies. And you can't copy the same materials from semester to semester. In other words, if you copied it last semester, you can't copy it again without getting permission from the copyright owner.

Computer Software

What can I copy?

Nothing…. without express written permission from the copyright holder. The one exception to this rule is that if you have purchased a copy of the software, you may make one backup copy of the original diskettes. This backup copy is only for emergency purposes and it may never be used unless the original copy is somehow destroyed or lost. The software may be copied onto the hard drive of a computer in order to run the program, but it is against the law to maintain simultaneous copies in different hard drives.

How many copies may I make?

Same as above. You may have only one backup copy of a computer program. Unless you have a license or other permission, you may not copy a computer program onto another computer. This includes loading a program into more than one computer by using one diskette intended for a single user.

Computer manuals and documentation are covered in the same manner as computer programs. You may not make multiple copies of computer documentation for classes. Copying a computer program intended for a single user onto a network is the same as making multiple copies of the program. It's a no-no. A network license is required to load a computer program onto a network, despite the fact that the program may, indeed, work in a network environment. So don't do it.

How long can I keep it?

As long as you own the program, you may keep a copy of a computer program on your hard drive and a backup copy in addition to the original diskettes or CD. If you should lose the copy on the hard drive, you may reload the program from the original or backup disks. If you sell or transfer the program to another person, you must transfer all diskettes and documentation to the new owner, and you must remove all copies of the program from your computer's hard drive and memory.

When and how may I use it?

Use of a computer program is usually governed by a license agreement, so it depends… Some licenses say you may freely make copies, others say you must pay a fee to use the software, or to install the software onto multiple machines. This is a contractual agreement and it supercedes the copyright restrictions.

You may not decompile a program and use program instructions in new programs. You may not defeat any form of copy protection built into the program. You may not use a single-user version of software on a network. You may not install a program on more than one computer at a time without express, written permission from the copyright owner. This means that you cannot install the program on your computer at home and your computer at school unless you own two copies of the program or have permission to do so from the copyright owner or the software license. Depending on the program, you may also be limited in what you can do with the output of the program. Some educational licenses restrict what you can do with computer output, or mark the output as educational material. You may not defeat these copy restrictions.

Music

What can I copy?

You may make emergency copies of music for an immediate performance, provided replacement copies have been ordered.

You may copy excerpts (not to exceed 10 percent of a work) provided they do not constitute a performable unit, and provided you make no more than one copy per student.

You may make a single recording of a copyrighted performance by students for evaluation purposes; it may be retained, but copies of it may not be made.

I have an old record. May I copy it to cassette and use that instead?

If the format of the record is obsolete (78 rpm, for example) and no other version is available, you may transfer the recording to a usable format. If the format is still available (33 1/3 rpm or 45 rpm) the transfer would require permission of the copyright holder. An exception allows you to make a single copy for the purpose of auditory exercises or examinations. You may retain the single copy made for such use.

My students are preparing a presentation for class and want to use parts of popular songs. Is this permissible?

If the presentation is created with multimedia software, the students may use up to 30 seconds of a popular song. If the presentation is anything other than multimedia, such use falls into a gray area. Student use is permitted if the students instigate the performance themselves (i.e., the students must decide on their own to use a specific song; the teacher may determine the suitability of the material, but may not tell the students to use a specific song.) The music students use should be played from legitimately purchased or borrowed recordings, or recorded off the air.

Index

A

AIME 55, 124, 133
administrator, role in copyright compliance 124, 127-131
amount of work copied 15
audiovisual materials 39-64
    entertainment showings 16, 42, 104, 130
    showings for reward 18, 42, 54, 104, 123, 130

B

backup copies 79
    video *See* video, archival copies
Berne Convention 4, 7, 111
Beta format videotape 47, 92
bounty hunters vii, 13
Business Software Alliance 84

C

CCG 94, 95
CCL 94, 95
cease and desist vii, 11-12, 34, 127
change of format *See* adaptation
chat 80, 116
closed circuit television 43
closed-captioning 62
common law copyright 8
computer software 77-88
    documentation 80
    lending 83
    license 77, 121-122
    public domain 83
CONFU 74, 100
Congressional Guidelines *See* fair use
consumable materials *See* print copying, consumables
contributory infringement *See* infringement, contributory
CONTU 93-99
conversion of obsolete formats 47
copiers
    unsupervised 21, 91
copies for physically handicapped 24
copying
    "bottom up" 17
copying in anticipation 17, 28
copyright
    corporate authorship 6
    damages 9
    duration 6-7
    enforcement 12
    penalties 9-10
    policy 11, 84, 133
    symbol *See* copyright notice
    unprotected works 3
copyright agent 113
Copyright Clearance Center 107
copyright management information 7, 22, 78
copyright notice 1-2, 3, 7, 37, 90
copyright police 11, 82
Copyright Software Rental Amendments Act 83
copyright symbol *See* copyright notice
copyright warning notices 7, 83, 90, 91
creative works 15

D

damaged or deteriorating materials 21, 32, 92
decision to copy 16-17
derivative works 4, 34, 48, 61, 62, 68
Digital Millennium Copyright Act 7, 22, 24, 73, 74, 79, 85, 90, 92, 95, 113,
display warning of copyright 7, 90, 94
distance learning 74

E

educational use 13-16
Electronic Communications Privacy Act 73
e-mail 114
essence of work 15

F

face-to-face teaching 41-45, 68, 74, 103
factual materials 3, 15
fair use 9, 13-19, 22-23
    audiovisual materials 39-43, 103
    brevity 25
    cumulative effect 26
    four tests 14-16
    guidelines 16
    multimedia 68-71
    proving 13
    spontaneity 26, 31
fax 97
fee for permission 105
film 52
fines 9, 128
financial impact of copying 15-16
fixation 1, 3, 7, 48, 116
format change *See* adaptation

G

general cultural value 42
graphics 60
    adaptation 60
    teacher-created 34

H

home use only *See* video, home use only
HTML 116

I

ideas
    copyright 1
illustrations
    copy limits 26
infringement 9-10
    contributory 10, 54, 60, 63, 79, 80, 86
    fines 9
    innocent 10, 89
    vicarious 11, 54, 80, 86-87
    willful 10
interlibrary loan 93-99
    rule of five 95-96
Internet 111-117
    links 115
    printing from 115
Internet service provider 113

L

library copying 21-22, 90
library exemptions 90
license
    shrink wrap 78, 104
links, Internet *See* Internet, links
local government documents
    copyright status 3

M

MARC records
    copyright control information 120
market for work 15-16
moral rights 6
multimedia 67-71
    copying 70
    fair use *See* fair use, multimedia
    quantity limits 69-70
    retention 68-69
music
    copying 35-36

N

National Commission on New Technological Uses
    of Copyrighted Works *See* CONTU
nature of protected work 14-15
networking 82
newsgroups
    fair use 114
No Electronic Theft (NET) Act 77
nonprofit use 144

O

obsolete materials 47, 92
off-air recording 54, 59
    retention 56
    taping rebroadcast 55
OSP *See* Internet service provider
out-of-print works 96

P

permissions 103-110
    time to receive 17, 32, 105
phonorecord 4
photocopying 4, 23-36, 90-92
    copy limits 23-36
    picture books 25
photographs 92, 111, 117
piracy 9, 74, 77, 78, 84
plagiarism 85
poetry
    copy limits 25
preservation 92
principal's
    liability 11
    role 119-120
print copying
    anthologies 23, 28, 32, 36, 37, 54, 70
    authority for 17, 24
    brevity 25
    consumables 17, 29
    cumulative effect 26-27
    frequency 17
    graphics 34
    interlibrary loan 33, 93
    multiple, for classrooms 25
    music 75
    periodicals 30
    replacing purchased materials 17
    reserve 33
    single, for teachers 23
    spontaneity 26, 31
    staff development 28